Database Management Systems

Database Management Systems

By

ARCHANA VERMA

GenNext Publication

First Published, 2018

Published by

GenNext Publication
5, Ansari Road
Daryaganj, New Delhi-110002
Phone: 9811692060
E-mail: gennextpublication@hotmail.com

Printed at: G. Print Process, Delhi.

Cataloging in Publication Data—DK
Courtesy: D.K. Agencies (P) Ltd. <docinfo@dkagencies.com>

Verma, Archana *(Associate professor)*, **author.**
Database management systems / by Archana Verma.
pages cm
ISBN 9789380223414

1. Database management—Textbooks. 2. Database management—India. I. Title.

LCC QA76.9.D3V47 2018 | DDC 005.74 23

Dedicated To

My Father
Sh. Vidya Sagar Verma

My Mother
Smt. Sudha Verma

My Sister
Dr. Vandana Verma Marwah

My Brother
Mr. Shashank Verma

My Brother-in-Law
Dr. Ashutosh Marwah

My Sister-in-Law
Mrs. Archana Devar Verma

My Daughter
Ritambhara

My Niece
Aparajita

My Nephew
Shreyas

My Cute Nephew
Kartikeya

Contents

Acknowledgement

I Deeply thank the Chairman, IEC Group of Institutions, Sh. R. L. Gupta for his blessings for writing this book.

I Truly thank the CEO, IEC Group of Institutions, Sh. Naveen Gupta for his encouragement and support.

I Sincerely thank the Director, IEC Group of Institutions, Prof. Sunil Kumar for his guidance and good wishes extended towards me.

I would like to thank the Director, Gyan Books Pvt.Ltd. Sh. Amit Garg and the staff members for publishing this book.

Lastly, I would like to thank my students for their appreciation of my notes which encouraged me to write this book.

AUTHOR

Synopsis

I was inspired to write this book when all my students appreciated my lectures and the way I teach. So I have tried to put the exaplations given in class and the examples explained on board in the form of a written material.

The book is primarily meant for B.Tech 3rd year students of Abdul Kalam Technical Univesrity Lucknow and various other universities for the Course of "DataBase Management System" can also use it. Suitable examples have been provided throughout the book for better comprehension. Also solved questions of ER Diagrams, Relational Algebra, SQL Queries and Functional Dependencies from previous years question papers have been provided in the book.

The book contains all the topics of Entity Relationship Model, Relational Model and Relational Algebra. SQL, Functional Dependencies and Normlization, Transaction processsing Concepts and Concurrency Control Techniques.

It is hoped that the students will benefit from this book and fare well in their exams. If they do, I will feel rewarded for the efforts.

AUTHOR

Chapter - 1

Introduction

1.1 An Overview of Database Management System

A data is raw facts or figures. A database is a collection of related data. If we put data in different files or at different places and they are not connected in any way or not related in any way then it is not a database. But a database is a collection where data are related to each other.

Suppose we are studying in a college, we have data about students, about teachers, about subjects stored separately, then they are not related, but if we put together the facts that which teacher teaches which student which subject then it is related data and it is a database.

A database may vary from small simple organizations like a college management system, a library management system to a little more sophisticated systems like airline reservation system, railway reservation system to a banking software. These are all examples of a database, for example you take the airline reservation system, then which flight goes to which city, how many seats are reserved, how many are vacant. All this information comes from the underlying database of an airline reservation system, where all the flight information, seat information is captured and stored together in related form and as the more number of passengers book tickets, the underlying database gets updated accordingly.

Now database from these commercial applications can also vary to very large databases where scientific applications are used for example, Bioinformatics, where information about a human genome is kept, so there are about 3 billion nucleotides in a human genome, for that you require vast amount of storage and special tools and interfaces to retrieve and process that information.

Also you require databases in scientific applications like weather forecasting and space navigation and robotics. SO there you need to store very large databases and supercomputers are required to process them.

So therefore the areas that a database covers range from very small to very large. Basically whenever you are using an application, the underlying data of how it is stored, arranged in a related way and manipulated and updated and retrieved and the correct answers displayed on the screen lead to the fact that a database management system is required.

The definitions of a few terms used in databases are as follows:

- A Database is a collection of related data.
- A Database Management System (DBMS) is a collection of programs that enables users to create and maintain a database.
- A data model is a collection of concepts that can be used to describe the structure of a database. By structure of database we mean what data types are used, what relationships exist between different entities and what different restrictions or constraints are put on the data.

1.2 Users in a Database System

The different users that use a database systems are of three types:

(1) DBA (Database Administrator)

(2) Database Designers

(3) End Users

(a) Casual

(b) Naïve

(c) Sophisticated
(d) Stand Alone

Let us describe each one's Role and Responsibilities in detail.

(1) The Database Administrator of the database is the chief administrator who has the overall control and responsibility of the Database. He has to manage the resources, provide or take away resources, grant permissions or take away permissions and see that the database is working correctly and efficiently. His main duties include:

   (a) Providing passwords and Login Ids to users for security reasons.

   (b) Seeing that the queries are giving the answers in a proper response time. If a query is taking a lot of time to execute, then find out the reason and fix it.

   (c) Coordinating and monitoring the overall use of the database that everything is running smoothly and to fix any problem if they arise.

   (d) Monitor the hardware and the software that is required for a database management system and to see and use it accordingly.

(2) The Database Designers are responsible for the designing of the database. They start from the first phase of software development life cycle to do requirements gathering and then do the analysis part and do the design by first drawing Data Flow Diagrams and Entity – Relationship diagrams to create the conceptual model of the database. They reduce the Entity Relationship diagram into tables. Also the database designers are responsible for defining the physical design of the database i.e. the storage structure. How the files will be organized, how the indexes will be organized, which storage structure to choose from, what would what would be best for query optimization etc. Because when we draw the Entity – Relationship diagram and from there we reduce it down to the tables. Then the tables become the file and the attributes become the fields of the file and the rows or tuples become the records of the files.

So therefore file organization is also important and needs to be decided.

(3) The 3rdtype of users are end users who simply use the database once everything is ready. The data has been put into the database and now they need to do the querying part of the database or manipulation of the database or modification of the database.

(a) The first category of casual users are those which belong to the managers who generally query the database for various types of inquiries to their level.

(b) The naïve type of users have limited access to the database, example bank tellers, reservation clerks for airlines and railways.

(c) The sophisticated type of users are engineers and scientists who do querying of very large databases and have to deal with sophisticated tools and databases interfaces for querying the database. Commercial type of databases are not found here.

(d) Stand Alone type of users are those who use databases which are made fpr a particular purpose. Example are Income Tax database and medical databases. In some countries, there are medical databases, so Doctors use that, and they put in the symptoms and other related information about the patients and get the diagnosis and the treatment required for that particular disease. Another example is the calculating of income tax of very large group of organizations. So chartered Accountants use that, they put in all the parameters related to tax calculation and get the result. Basically the stand alone systems cannot be used by anyone, they are for a particular purpose and the expert of that field will be able to understand it and use it.

1.3 Database Systems vs File systems

Let us compare a database system and a file system which was used earlier to store the data. Let us see the advantages that a Database system has over a file system.

These are the following advantages:

(1) Data Redundancy and Inconsistency:The problem of data being redundant (or duplicate) and stored in ecause the different files and thereby giving chance for data to become inconsistent exists more in a file system than a Database Management System. In aq database Management System. The name of an employee (for example) would be stored in one place that is in the employees table along with the empid as its primary key, and suppose the name changes (a lady gets married and wishes to change her surname now). So in that case it will only be changed at one place in the employee table and any references to that problem of inconsistency because the data is not stored in too many places. It is only at one place in the employee table. But compare it to earlier file systems where there may be 3 files containing the name of the person and if for any reason we change it at 2 places and forget to change at the 3rd place or the system has accidently been shut down. Then at 2 places there would be a different surname and at a 3rd place there would be a different surname leading to inconsistent data.

(2) Difficulty in Accessing Data: In a file processing system it is difficult to write queries such as 'Give me the names of the employees who live in a particular city and are drawing a salary between 30000 and 50000'. In file systems it may be possible that one file is having the personal information of the employee that is his address and another file is having the professional information of the employee that is his salary etc. So picking up values from different files in real time becomes a problem, whereas in a database systems such queries are easily answered.

(3) Data Isolation: Some of the fields may be placed in one file other fields may be placed in another file and the data would be scattered in different files. In a DBMS the data is related together by relationships and connected for easier and quicker access.

(4) Integrity Problems: We cannot put restrictions in a file on the values that we are putting in a a particular field, whereas in

a DBMS we can have restrictions put on a field, for example in Age we can say that put values between 18 and 80, we cannot have a child working and we cannot have a senior citizen working. So we can put restrictions or limitations in columns.

(5) Atomicity Problems: The transactions in a Database Management System occur in its entirety or none at all. Because if a transaction is failed in the middle, we do not allow it to execute further and complete itself, rather we rollback and restart it with original values rolling back the values it had changed.

(6) Security Problems; Not everybody is allowed to access the database, there are proper logins and passwords set and distributed by the database administrator to authorize users. But in a file system, we cannot put restrictions on who is accessing the files or not. Very few operating systems provide access restrictions on files.

1.4 Categories of Data Models

The data models are made according to the type of concepts that they depict and the type of database structure they describe.

There are 2 main categories of a data model.

(1) High Level or Conceptual

(2) Low level or Physical

The high level or conceptual data model is based on the fact that how the users look at the database from their point of view.

The low level or physical data model is based on the fact that how a computer looks at the database from its point of view, it is mainly concerned with how to store the data in the database.

Conceptual data model needs to be described with the help of some definitions given below:

(1) Entity: An entity is a real world object or thing which describes a particular object such as student,employee,course or patient.

(2) Attribute: An attribute is some characteristic that describes an entity such as the name of the student or his Roll_No, the

Subject code of a course, the Salary of an employee or the address of a patient.

(3) Relationship: This exists between two entities and it depicts the fact that how the two entities are related to each other. For example a student studies a course. So Studies is a relationship between two entities student and Course. An EMPLOYEE works in a DEPARTMENT. So works is a relationship between two entities EMPLOYEE and DEPARTMENT. A DOCTOR treats a PATIENT. So treats is a relationship between DOCTOR and PATIENT.

There are a couple of more definitions that need to be described before we are finally able to describe a Data Model and they are as follows:

Schemas, Instances and Database States

(4) Schema: The description of the database is known as the database schema. It mainly tells us what are going to be the names of the tables or (Relations). What are going to be the columns or attributes in that table.

(5) Instance: The instance of the database is the data that composes the rows and columns in the database at any given time is the instance of the database. It is also known as the **database state** or the snapshot of the database. Compare this to a person who is taking photographs of his kids. At one time, the kids are standing in a particular pose. In another picture the kids would be standing differently. Similarly is the case with the **snapshot of the database**, at one time the employee details may be different. Suppose his address changes and he gets increment in salary, then the values inside the columns for tat particular employee will be different before and after. So this is the instance of the database, that at one time the rows and columns would be occupying different values and at other times, the rows and columns would be occupying different values.

(6) Intension of the Database: This is the same as the schema of the database.

(7) Extension of the Database: This is the same as the Database State or the data inside the rows and columns at any time, also

known as Instance of the database or the snapshot of the database.

Let us take an example to explain the above terms:

Schema or Intension of the Database:

EMPLOYEE

Empid	Name	Address	Fathers_Name	Salary

COURSE

Course_Code	Course_Name	Credits	Branch	Level

So the schema describe the structure of the database, that is just the names of tables and the fields inside the table.

Database State or the Extension of the Database

Empid	**Name**	**Address**	**Fathers_Name**	**Salary**
10001	Amit	MayurVihar	Vijay Raj	20000
10002	Preeti	Dwarka	GopalNath	30000
10003	Gita	InderPuri	Rama Chandra	40000
10004	Deepa	Tilak Nagar	Krishan Kumar	50000

→ **Schema**

DataBase State at one point of time.

EMPLOYEE

Empid	**Name**	**Address**	**Fathers_Name**	**Salary**
10001	Amit	Vasundhara	Vijay Raj	25000
10002	Preeti	Dwarka	GopalNath	30000
10003	Gita	Vaishali	Rama Chandra	40000
10004	Deepa	Tilak Nagar	Krishan Kumar	55000

→ **Schema**

DataBase State at another Point of time.

1.5 The 3 Schema Architecture

The three schema architecture has 3 levels:

(1) The Internal Level

(2) The Conceptual Level

(3) The External or View Level

(1) The Internal Level: This level of schema uses the low level Data Model or the Physical Data Model the describe how we store the Data and in what structure on the disk. It is basically related to the physical design and storage of the database which the Database Designers had done while preparing how the files will be organized and how they will be indexed etc.

(2) The Conceptual Level: This level of schema uses the conceptual model to describe how the would look like to the user. It covers the whole structure of the database by describing it in terms of the entities, attributes and the relationships which will be used, the datatypes and the constraints which will be used. Normally this uses the Entity-Relationship (ER) Model as its base. The ER model will be discussed in the next chapter. This level does not describe the physical storage details.

(3) The External or the View Level: This level exists at the top most level for the user. It hides all physical storage details and conceptual design of the database also. It only provides the reports to the users or the answers which will be shown to the users by hiding all lower level details.

The following diagram shows the structure of the 3 schema architecture:

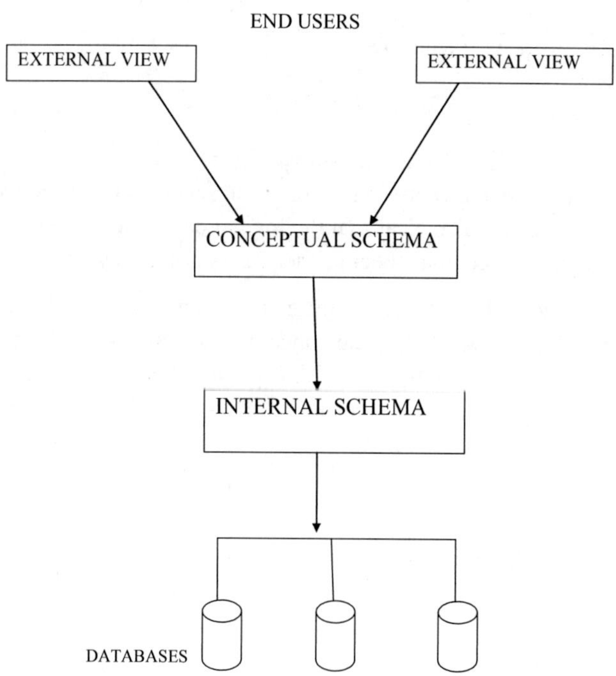

1.6 Data Independence

The Data Independence mechanism occurs between the layers of the 3 level schema architecture. It is defined as if we change the schema at a lower level, then the upper level schema does not get affected.

There are 2 types of Data Independence:

(1) Logical Data Independence

(2) Physical Data Independence

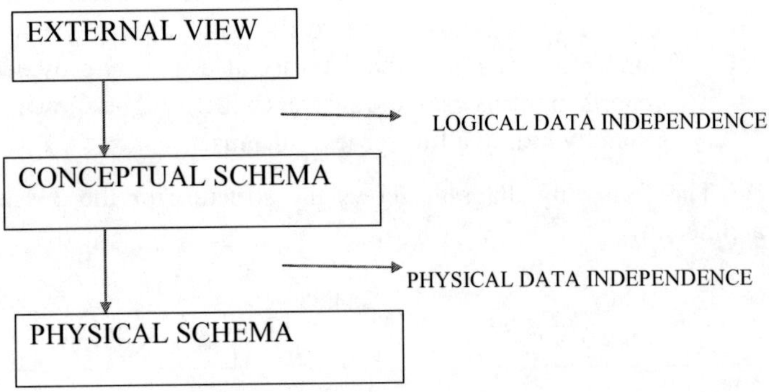

As it is clear from the above figure that the physical data independence occurs between the physical schema and the conceptual schema. And it is also clear that the logical data independence occurs between the conceptual schema and the external view.

(1) Logical Data Independence: The Logical Data Independence is defined as, if we change the conceptual schema, then the external schema remains the same. The Conceptual Schema means the tables which have been made from the ER Diagram, if changed will not affect the report or the external view. The report will show the answers as they were showing before changing the conceptual schema.

Let us take an example to demonstrate this. Suppose our conceptual schema has the following tables.

COURSE

COURSE_NO	*COURSE_NAME*
CS401	DBMS
CS402	OS
CS403	DAA
CS404	CN

STUDENT

STUDENT_NO	*STUDENT_NAME*
11	Shashi
29	Pooja
9	Pragya
20	Aarti

GRADE

STUDENT_NO	*COURSE_NO*	*GRADE*
11	CS403	A
29	CS404	C
9	CS401	A
20	CS403	B
20	CS401	A
9	CS402	B

The external schema is as follows:

STUDENT NAME	*STUDENT GRADE REPORT*		
	COURSE_NO	*GRADE*	*COURSE_NAME*
Shashi	CS403	A	DAA
Pooja	CS404	C	CN
Pragya	CS401	A	DBMS
Pragya	CS402	B	OS
Aarti	CS401	A	DBMS
Aarti	CS403	B	DAA

Now suppose we change our conceptual schema as follows:

STUDENT_NO	*STUDENT_NAME*	*COURSE_NO*	*COURSE_NAME*	*GRADE*
11	Shashi	CS403	DAA	A
9	Pragya	CS401	DBMS	A
9	Pragya	CS402	OS	B
20	Aarti	CS401	DBMS	A
20	Aarti	CS403	DAA	B
29	Pooja	CS404	CN	C

Now in our above conceptual schema Redundancy exists. As there is only one table, the earlier one with 3 tables was better that it had no redundancies.

But anyway by changing the conceptual schema we do not change the external view and our report of the external view still remains the same as:

STUDENT NAME	***STUDENT GRADE REPORT***		
	COURSE_NO	***GRADE***	***COURSE_NAME***
Shashi	CS403	A	DAA
Pooja	CS404	C	CN
Pragya	CS401	A	DBMS
Pragya	CS402	B	OS
Aarti	CS401	A	DBMS
Aarti	CS403	B	DAA

(2) Physical Data Independence: As was shown earlier in the diagram, the physical data independence is between the layers of physical schema and conceptual schema. So that it means changing the lower level layer that is the physical schema should not affect our conceptual schema. Because we always change the lower level layer and it should not affect the upper level layer. This means that if we change our way of file organization, that is from random to indexed or to indexed sequential or any other. Then our tables and the attributes in them will remain the same. There will be no change in the conceptual schema, that is all the table names and the attributes with their data types will remain as it were. The data inside the tables will also remain the same that is the schema and the database state will remain as it is. The intension of the database and the extension of the database will remain the same only the storage structure will change at the physical storage level.

1.7 DataBase Languages and Interfaces

There are 4 types of database Languages:

(1) Data Definition Language (DDL)

(2) Data Manipulation Language (DML)

(3) View Definition Language (VDL)

(4) Storage Definition Language (SDL)

Let us describe each one in detail.

(1) The Data Definition Language is used by the Database Designers to define the schema of the database. That is when the ER diagram is reduced into the tables, then the database designers decide what tables should exist, what should their names be, what attributes each table should have, what its datatypes should be and what constraints are to be put.

The Data Definition Language has the commands like:

(a) CREATE TABLE – to create a table.

(b) ALTER TABLE – to add or delete an attribute from a table.

(c) DROP TABLE – to remove the table from database

So this language changes the schema or the intension of the database.

(2) Data Manipulation Language: This language is used by the end users to query the database and to manipulate the database state or the extension of the database. By Manipulation we mean that new records in the database can be inserted records or rows can be deleted, a particular field inside a particular row can be modified. The various queries can be put.

The Data Manipulation Language has the commands like:

(a) INSERT INTO – to insert a row

(b) DELETE FROM – to delete a row or a couple of rows

(c) UPDATE - to modify a particular attribute for a particular row.

(d) SELECT
FROM
WHERE - to query the database.

(3) Storage Definition Language – This language is used by the Database Designers to decide how the files will be organized into disks. It is going to be random method, indexed method or indexed sequential method etc. This is the language used at internal level of schema.

(4) The View Definition language is used to create views. These views are like reports. They do not take any storage space but

take values from the data inside the tables and views are created and stored in database so that when that particular report is required, we need not create the view again but use the stored view and run it. This is the language used at external level of schema.

The Data Manipulation language are divided into two types:

(1) High Level DML

(2) Low Level DML

High Level DML is Non-Procedural

Low Level DML is Procedural

(1) High Level DML is one which does not require any host language, it can run on its own on a Data Base Management System. For example SQL is a high level DML which can run on a DBMS like Oracle or any version of Oracle e.g. Oracle 10g.

(2) Low Level DML is a language which cannot run on its own, it requires a host language to run on. For example PL/SQL is a low level DML which requires a high level language to run on. So PL/SQL normally uses C as its Host Language and then we can run C program with SQL embedded it.

Our SQL contains DDL, DML and VDL commands, but it does not contain SDL commands. So DML packages like SQL etc contain the above mentioned 3 languages.

DATABASE INTERFACES

We have the following Type of interfaces to use the DML.

(1) Menu Based Interfaces for banking System.

(2) Form Based Interfaces for displaying forms

(3) Natural Language Interfaces which can recognize voice and languages like English to understand and act accordingly.

(4) Interfaces for Parametric Users: Example – Bank Tellers, Reservation Clerks of Airlines and Railways that have access to small set of operations.

(5) DBA Interfaces – which have access to privileged set of commands.

(6) GUI – Using Mouse point and Click.

(7) Scientific Tools: such as FASTA, BLAST in Bioinformatics to access genome sequences. Other scientific projects would require their own set of scientific tools.

1.8 DataBase Structure:

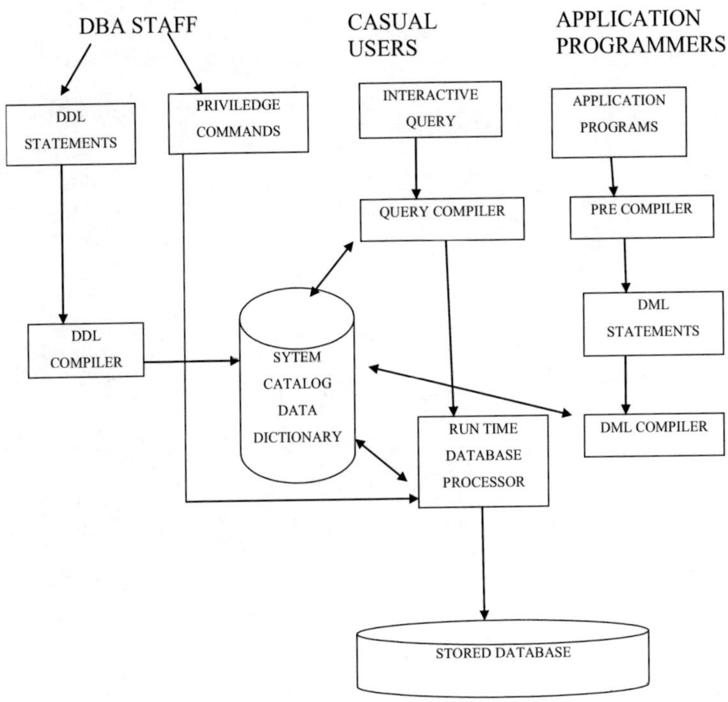

The above diagram shows how users and compilers act together to process the data and pass to the stored database.

Chapter - 2

Entity Relationship Model

2.1 Definitions

The Entity Relationship Model is used to describe the conceptual schema or the way a user would perceive the entire view of his database.

Later on this model is reduced into tables using the technique of Normalization so that Redundancies and inconsistencies are removed and those tables would ultimately form the database.

We need to describe certain terms again for the ER model as the name suggests Entity Relationship Model.

(1) ***Entity***: An Entity is a real world object or thing which can exist on its own independently. This particularly describes a noun, a person, an object or thing which has some form of physical existence. e.g. STUDENT, VEHICLE, DEPARTMENT.

(2) ***Attribute***: Each enity has a set of attributes which are the characteristics or properties which describe that entity. e.g. if we have an entity PERSON then he may be described by attributes such as his name, address, date_of_birth, phone_ no etc.

Now the attributes are of many types. We will describe ech one in detail.

(a) ***Single and Composite Attributes***: A single attribure is a imple atribute which takes one value e.g. salary of a person is a

single value. A person may be drawing one amount of salary and that would be his figure.

A composite attribute on the other hand is one that can be broken down into smaller attributes with independent meanings.

For example, name can be considered as a composite attribute. It can be broken down into first name and last name. Similarly address can be a composite attribute. It can be broken down into house_no, street_no, area, city, state, pincode etc.

It entirely depends upon the databvase designers to choose whether attributes which can be made composite are to be represented as single attributes or composite attributes depending upon the requirements of the user. Some applications may require that you store first name and last name seperately for easier searches, wheres other applications may not require. Similarly is the case with address, we can store it as a single attribute but some applications may require that you store city, state seperately. So in that case we have to show address as a composite attribute.

Attributes which cannot be divided further are called atomic or simple attributes.

(b) ***Single Valued vs Multivalued Attributes:*** Single valued attributes are those which have only one value for their attribute, e.g. name of a department. A departmen is going to have one name and not multiple names.

Mulivalued attribute are those which can have multiple vvalues for their attributes, e.g. phone number. A person may have 2 or 3 phone numbers. Similarly qualification can be multivalued attribute. Some people may have one qualification such as B.Tech whereas others may have multiple qualifications such as B.Tech, M.tech, P.hd.

(c) ***Stored vs derived attributes:*** stored attributes are those in which when we put a value, it is stored there and when we exract or retrieve that value, it comes back as it is. Derived attributes are those in which we put a value and it can calculate some other attribute using some parameters. For example,

compare date_of_Birth as an attribute and age as an attribute. Now here Age is a derived attribute, because age can be calculated from the system date. we take the year part of the date_of_birth, compare it will the year part of the system date (which is the current date) an claculate the age of the person. Date_of_Birth is a stored attribute. We put a date in date_of_birth attribute and simple extract that date of birth.

Null Values: Null Values are those when we do not have a value for an attribute, instead of leaving it blank we fill it with NULL, so that we tell the system tht the attribute has no value and we have safely put a value NULL, so that by mistake other values are not entered into it.

Why would we need a NULL value? Suppose you have an attribute qualification and University paased from. Now here qualification means degrees after 12th standard. So if there is an employee table and it has attributes qualification and unversity, then for a person like peon, who is still an employee of your organization does not have a college degree and has not passed from any university. He is just passed 10th standard. Then you will have to safely put the values of Null in the qualification column and the university column for that person peon.

(d) ***Complex Attributes:*** Complex attributes are those which are a combination of composite and Multivalued attributes.

2.2 Entity Types, Entity Sets and Value Sets

Till now we have described an entity as a real world object or thing. Now we are going to distinguish between the entity types, entities and the entity sets.

An Entity Type is what we have been calling an entity till now. A real world object or thing is an entity-type. For example A STUDENT is an Entity Type.

The individual tudents who are studying are entities now.

So the Entity Type is an Abstract thing which does not have any values. But the entities are the actual students who have a paricular value like his Roll-No, Name, Father's-Name Address etc.

And an Entity Set is the set of all those entities which make up the student table or all the students taken together is an entity set.

Let us take an example to illustrate this.

STUDENT ←Entity Type

Roll_No	*Name*	*Address*	*Father_Name*	
10001	Gita	Mayur Vihar	Jagan Mohan	<-Entity
10002	Pawan	Gurgaon	Deena Nath	<-Entity
10003	Preeti	Janak Puri	Gopal Das	<-Entity
10004	Deepa	Tilak Nagar	Rama Chandra	<-Entity
10005	Amit	Laxmi Nagar	Krishan Kumar	<-Entity
10006	Gita	Inder Puri	Vijay Pandit	<-Entity

} Entity Set

Value Sets: The values that a particular attribute is going to take from a value set or a domain.

For Example, we can easily see that our Roll_No in above table is taking only digits. So its domain or value set is digits and other three attributes (name, address, Father_name) are taking alphabets, so their domain or value sets is alphabets.

2.3 Keys

A key attribute is one which is unique in the table, and using that key attribute you can find the details of that particular entity or record. From the above table, we see that Roll_No is unique for each Entity, whereas other attributes may or may not be unique. We have two people with the same name Gita and these two persons with the name Gita are having different Roll_nos. So here Roll_No qualifies to be the key attribute and Name cannot become the key attribute since it is not unique. Similarly two persons may be living at the same address, if they are brothers and studying in the same college, so address cannot be a key attribute, but their Roll_nos will be different. For Similar reasons, Father_Name cannot be unique, there may be two students whose Father's Name match.

There are 4 Types of Keys:

(1) Primary Key

(2) Super Key

(3) Canidate Key

(4) Foreign Key

A **Primary Key** is one which has the property of the key and is used in the table to identify the rows uniquely. Because a table may have more than one key, but we make Primary Key as the one which is responsible for retrieving the rows uniquely. E.g. Roll_No of a student is the Primary Key of the STUDENT table.

A **Candidate Key** is a key which is eligible to become a Primary Key that is it has all the properties to become a Primry Key. This means when a table has more than one key then they are all Candidate Keys. E.g. a Department Table may have Dept_Number and Dept_Name as attributes and both these attributes contain unique values. A Dept_Number will be different for each Department and The names of the Departments will also be unique and therefore both atributes satisfy the property of a key. So both are Candidate Keys and we will choose one of them to become the Primary Key.

A **Super Key** is a key plus combination of other attributes in the table. E.g. Roll_No, Name is a Superkey. Roll_no Name, Address is also a superkey for the STUDENT table taken above.

A **Foreign Key** is one which appears in one table and refrences the Primary Key of another Table. For Example we have the STUDENT table which has Roll_No as its Primary Key. And now we have another table STUDYING as folows:

STUDYING

Roll_No	Course_Id	Grade

The STUDYING table tells us which student is studying which course and he got what grade in it.

So the Roll_No in the STUDYING table is the Foreign Key Which references the Primary Key Roll_No of STUDENT table.

Note that there is another table existing with the name of COURSE and it has details about each course in whih the Primary key of the COURSE table is Course_Id. So the course_id attribute of STUDYING table is a Foreign key and reference the Primary key Course_Id of COURSE table.

2.4 Relationships, Relationship Types, Relationship Instance, Relationship Sets, Relationship Degree

A Relationship occurs when two Entity Types interact. For example, when a student studies a COURSE. Then STUDENT and COURSE are entity types and STUDIES is a Relationship between them.

A **Relationship Type** is a **Relationship** that exists between two enity types. For exmple, we have the enity types STUDENT and COURSE as follows an the Relationship Type STUDIES as follows:

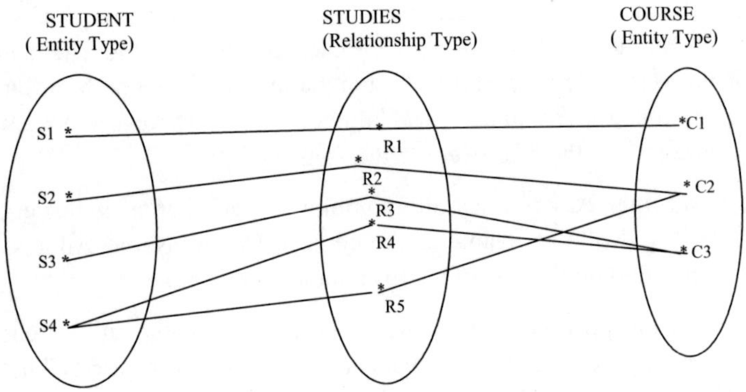

Now S1, S2, S3 and S4 are the entities of the entity type STUDENT. {S1, S2, S3, S4} make the entity set for the STUDENT Entity type.

C1, C2 and C3 are the entities of the entity type COURSE. {C1, C2, C3} make the entity set for the COURSE entity type.

The **Reltionship Instances** are R1, R2, R3, R4 and R5 which indicate which particular student studies which particular course. {R1, R2, R3, R4, R5} make the **Relationship Set** for the relationship type STUDIES.

Relationship Degree: The degree of the Relationship Type means how many Entity Types participate in a Relationship Type. For example

Relationship Degree =2

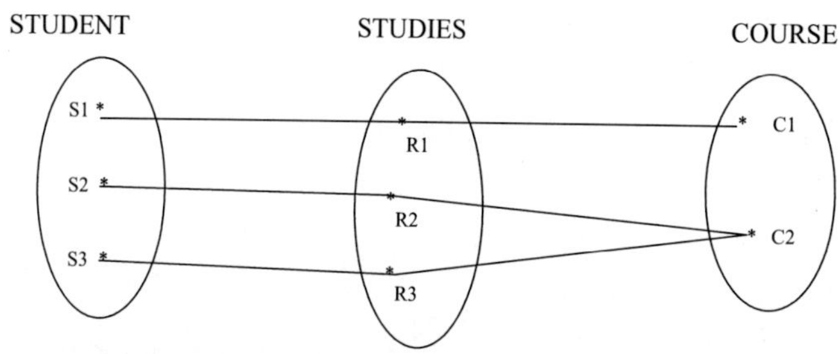

Relationship Degree =3

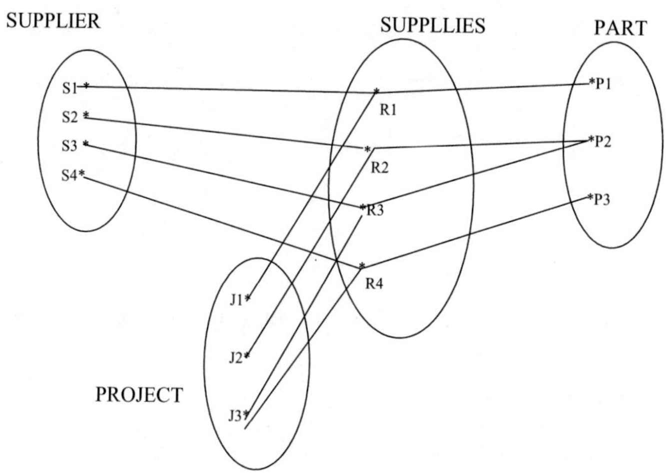

In Relationship Degree=2, each relationship instance has 2 entities participating in it.

In Relationship Degree = 3, each relationship instance has 3 entities participating in it.

2.4.1 Recursive Relationships

Suppose we have a PROFESSOR as an entity type, who is working and another entity type PROFESSOR is one who works above him or heads him.

Then the two enity types that participate in a Relationship Type are the same. Both are profesors because one works under him and the other works above him.

Basically there are 2 roles that the entity types are playing. One is head and the other is subordinate.

So the Relationship instances exist as follows:

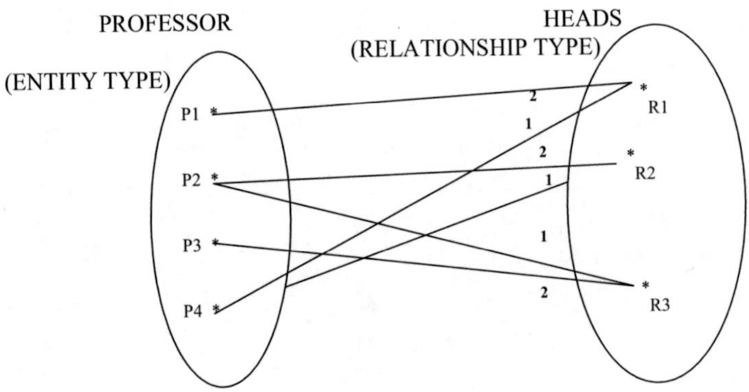

Role 1 indicates that this professor is the head of the professor who is shown by role 2.

Role 1 = Head

Role 2 = Subordinate

For example, let us take the 1st relationship instance R1. In this P1 participate as role 2 and P4 participates as role 1. So P4 Professor is the head of the Professor P1.

This type of Relationship is called Recursive Relationship. When both Entity Types that participate in a Relationship Type are the same with 2 different roles.

2.5 Constraints on Relationship Types

There are two types of constraints which exist on the Relationship Type.

(1) Cardinality Ratio

(2) Participation Constraint

(1) **2.5.1 CARDINALITY RATIO**: The Cardinality Ratio constraint says that in how many relationship instances an entity can participate in.

There are 3 types of Cardinality Ratio Constraints or relationship types

(a) 1: 1

(b) 1:N

(c) M:N

(a) The **1:1** Relationship says that one entity from one entity type and only another one entity from another entity type participate in a relationship instance.

For example there are two entity types, DEPARTMENT and PROFESSOR and they have a relationship MANAGES. So a professor will manage only one department and one department will be managed by only one professor. So from both sides of the entity types, there are single entities participating in the relationship type.

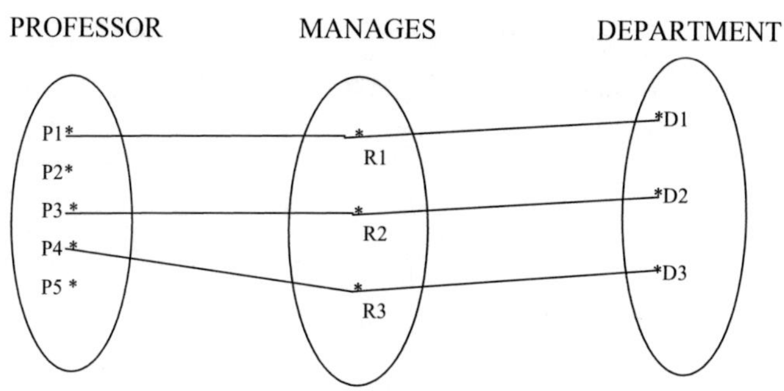

(b) In a **1:N** constraint, there are two entity types, and from one entity type, a single entity is participating in a relationship instance and from another entity type, a single entity participates in more than one relationship instance.

For Example, there are STUDENT and DEPARTMENT entity types and they participate in a relationship type BELONGS. One student belongs to one department, but a department may have a number of students belonging to it.

So the relationship is captured as follows:

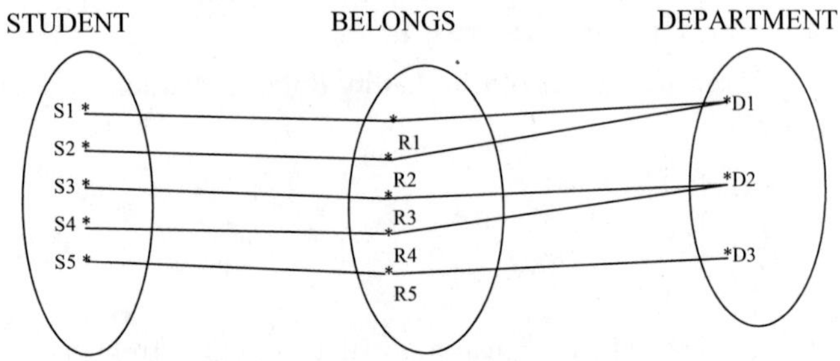

(c) In a **M:N** Relationship, there are two entity types. From one entity type, a single entity participates in more than one relationship instance. From the other entity type, a single entity also participates in more than one relationship instance.

For example, let us take two entity types STUDENT and COURSE and there is a relationship type STUDIES which exists between them. So a single student may study many courses and a single course may be studied by many students.

So the relationship is captured as follows:

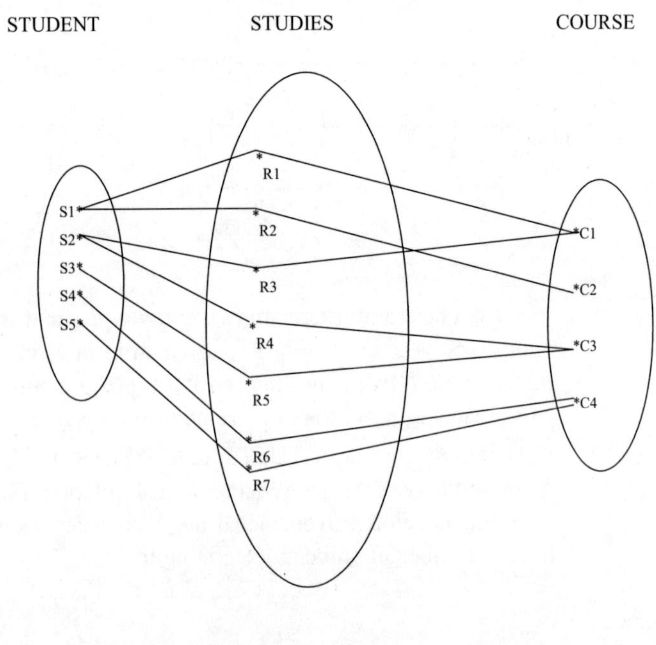

(2) 2.5.2 PARTICIPATION CONSTRAINT : There are two types of Participation Contraints and they are;

(a) Total

(b) Partial

(a) Total: In a total participation constraint, the existence of an entity in an entity type depends whether it participates in a relationship type or not. If it participates in a Relationship Type, then it can exist, if it does not participate in a particular relationship type, then it cannot exist.

For example, consider our Relationship Belongs and the entity types STUDENT and DEPARTMENT. If a particular student does not belong to any department, then he cannot exist in the college, because for studying you have to take up a degree of a particular department.

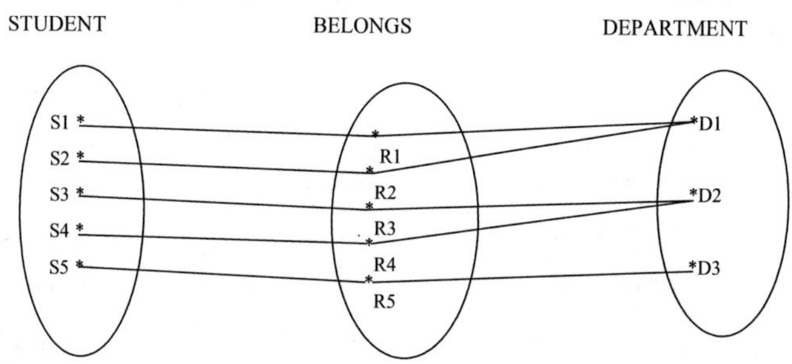

Here the students {S1, S2, S3, S4, S5} belong to some department or the other.

(b) Partial: In a partial contraint, the existence of an enity in an entity type does not depend that it has to participate in particular relationship type. It may participate in the Relationship Type or it may not participate in the relationship type.

For example, consider our manages relationship type and entity types PROFESSOR and DEPARTMENT . Now for a department you must have a manager. But it is not essential that every professor is a manager. The professor table or entity type will consist of all the professors in the college, but only some of them will be managing some departments. The rest still exist in the college. So the existence of the profesor does not depend whether he participates in the relationship instance of the relationship type manages.

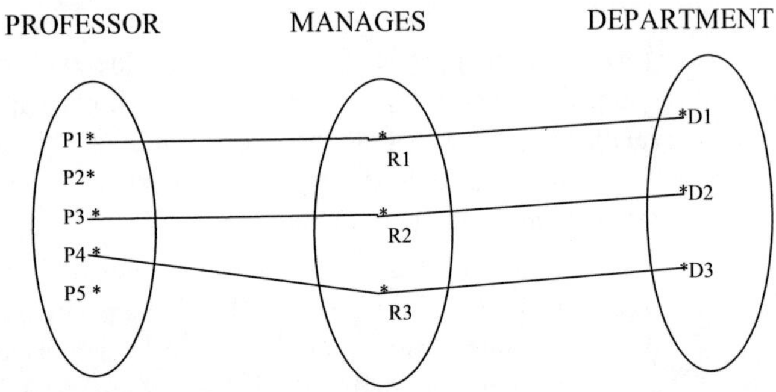

Attributes of Relationship Types: Till now we have seen that our attributes exist in the relations or tables and from there they take different values and form the records.

Whenever we have an M:N Relationship, there may be some attributes which belong to the relationship type. Because that attribute cannot be put on either of the 2 entity types.

So that attribute is of the relationship type and will exist in the new relation, which will be created in an M:N relationship.

Let us take our example of an M:N relationship. STUDENT and COURSE are entity types and the STUDIES is the M:N Relationship Type between the two entity types. Now this indicates which student studies which course and what all courses are studied by which students. So if we have a grade attribute, then this particular grade is of a particular student who got this grade in a particular course. So this attribute cannot be migrated either to the entity type STUDENT or entity type COURSE.

This fact will be more clear when we reudce our ER diagram into tables.

2.6 The ER Diagram

To draw an Entity Relationship Diagram, first we should have the requirements gathered by the database designers for any application say Railway Reservation System or any Banking Application etc.

Here if we want to darw an ER diagram of a simple college database. Then we need to specify the requirements. Make the ER diagram and reduce it into tables. The requirements of a college database are as folows:

(1) A student studies in a college. His student Id, Name and address are captured.

(2) There are a number of Professors who work in the college, their Name,ID, salary and which department they belong to is captured.

(3) There are students who study a number of courses and the grade they got in that course is also captured.

(4) A professor can teach a number of courses.

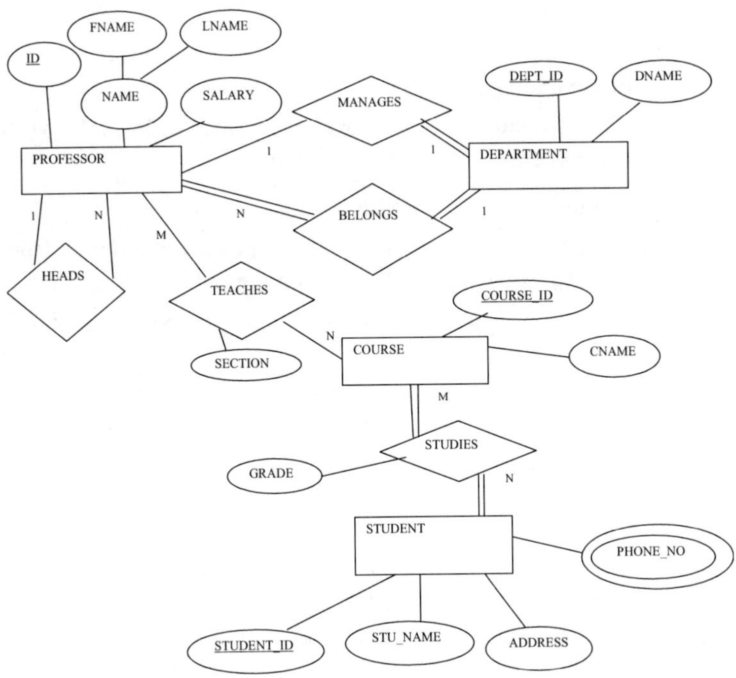

(5) The details about a particular course are also captured, its course id, and the name of the course.

(6) A professor may also be heded by another professor.

The conventions used in an ER diagram are as follows:

(1) An Entity Type is shown by a Rectangle.

(2) An Attribute is shown by an Oval

(3) A Relationship is shown by a Diamond.

(4) A composite Attribute is shown by an oval and its subordinate attributes emerging as ovals from it.

(5) A multivalued attribute is shown as a double oval.

(6) A recursive relationship is shown between a single entity type with both lines pointing to that entity type.

(7) A total participation constraint is shown by double lines between the relationship and the entity type.

(8) A partial constraint is shown by a single line between the entity type and the relationship.

(9) An attribute of a relationship is shown by the oval coming out of the diamond.

(10) The cardinaliy ratio constraints are written as 1:1, 1:M, M: N on each entity side.

Now let us describe the ER diaagram given above.

- The name of the professor is a composite attribute. So from one oval, two other ovals are coming out.
- The phone_no of a student is a multivalued attribute, so shown by double oval.
- The professor may or may not manage a department so single line between professor and manages. (Partial Constraint)
- The department must be manged by a professor. So double line between the manges relationship and department entity type. (Total Constraint)
- The professor may or may not head another professor. So single line between professor and heads relationship. A professor may or may not be headed by another professor, because suppose the Director of the college is also a professor

but nobody is on top of him. So single line again between professor and heads relationhip.

- A professor must belong to a department. A department must have professors belonging to it otherwise they cannot exist. So double lines between professor and belongs relationship type. And double lines between department and belongs relationship type.
- The professor may or may not teach a course, for example the Director does not need to teach a course. A course may or may not be taught by some professor, because it may be elective, may be taught next year or next semester.
- The course may or may not be studied by a student. But a student must study at least one course otherwise he cannot be a student.

The cardinality ratio constraints are explained.

- A professor may head a number of professors but a professor will be headed by only one professor . so 1:N is shown between heads relationship.
- A professor will manage only one department and a department will be managed by only one professor so 1:1 constraint between manages relationship.
- A department may have a number of professors belonging to it, so N is on the side of the professor entity type and belong relationship type. A professor can belong to only one department. So 1 is on the side of the department entity type and belongs relationship type.
- A professor may teach a number of courses and a course may be taught by a number of professors in different sections. So M and N an be placed on any side of the professor and teaches relationship type and teaches and course entity type. So Sections is going to be an attribute of the relationship type teaches because it does not belong to either the entity type professor (because it is not describing any property of the professor) or the entity type course (because it is not describing any property of the course either). But it is describing which

professor teaches which course in which section. So it is the attribute of the relationship type teaches.

- A particular course may be studied by a number of students. So M or N can be put on the student side between studies relationship type. A student may study a number of courses so N (if M was on student side) or M (if N was on the student side) can be put on the course side of the enity type and between studies relationship type.

2.7 Reducing the ER Diagram into Tables

In an ER diagram, the attributes of an entity type must be shown as attributes of a table and the relationship types also have to be captured as attributes of the table.

Because ultimately tables will be reduced to file records for physical storage. So we need to put everything in the form of attributes of a table, all attributes and all relationships.

We will first reduce the entity types and then go on to relationships.

Let us take the PROFESSOR entity type first.

It has Id, salary as its attributes and name is a composite attribute, So the composite atribute will be broken down into sub attributes and then the PROFESSOR table will be as follows.

PROFESSOR

Id	Fname	Lname	Salary

Now Id will become the key, because it uniquely identifies a professor. So by convention it is underlined.

Let us take the DEPARTMENT entity type.

It has only two attributes Dept_Id and Dname. The table Department becomes as follows with the key Dept_Id since it can uniquely identify the department.

DEPARTMENT

Dept_Id	Dname

Let us take the COURSE entity type.. It has 2 attributes Course_Id and Cname

The table course becomes as follows with the key Course_Id since it can uniquely identify the course.

COURSE

Course_Id	Cname

Let us take the STUDENT entity type. It has Student_Id, Stu_Name, Address and Phone_No as attributes. So the table is as follows with Student_Id as primary key.

STUDENT

Student_Id	Stu_Name	Address	Phone_No

But Phone_No is a multivalued attribute. So it will have multiple values, the records may look somewhat like this.

STUDENT

Student_Id	***Stu_Name***	***Address***	***Phone_No***
10001	Amit	Mayur Vihar	9818024665, 9818010007
10002	Deepa	Vasant Vihar	9818005607, 9814456070, 01203297643
10003	Gita	Vasant Kunj	9818066550
10004	Pawan	Shivalik	9818044556, 9818043567, 01166775544

This is not allowed. For a databse only a single value can exist in a single row, single column.

So we will have to decompose the table into 2 tables. We will remove the multivalued attribute that is causing the problem from the first table and we will have 2 tables as follows.

STUDENT

Student_Id	Stu_Name	Address

STUDENT_PHONES

Student_Id	Phone_No

The Student_id attribute is in both tables so that if we want the name of a student and his phone number we can access both tables and join them on the student_id attribute to retrieve the data.

Now Student_Id is enough to be the key of the STUDENT table because it will uniquely identify the records of the STUDENT table.

But Student_id cannot become the key of the STUDENT_PHONES table because of the following reason.

Let us see how our tables will look like if we use the same database state given above.

Our STUDENT table will look like this:

STUDENT

Student_Id	*Stu_Name*	*Address*
10001	Amit	Mayur Vihar
10002	Deepa	Vasant Vihar
10003	Gita	Vasant Kunj
10004	Pawan	Shivalik

And our STUDENT_PHONES will look like this

STUDENT_PHONES

Student_Id	*Phone_No*
10001	9818024665
10001	9818010007
10002	9818005607
10002	9814456070
10002	01203297643
10003	9818066550
10004	9818044556
10004	9818043567
10004	01166775544

So here the Student_Id attribute is not unique, but the combination of the attributes {student_id, phone_no} make the row unique. So therefore here our key will be {Student_Id, Phone_No} and the table will look like this.

STUDENT_PHONES

Student_Id	Phone_No

So whenever there is a multivalued attribute. It has to be decomposed into another table.

Now we have looked at each enity and its attributes. Now we have to look at relationships to convert them into attributes.

Let us first take the relationship MANAGES. Now to convert MANAGES relationship into an attribute, either the key attribute of department table must be put into the professor table or the key attribute of professor table must be put into the department table. So we can have either of the 2 tables given below:

PROFESSOR

Id	Fname	Lname	Salary	Dept_Id

Or

DEPARTMENT

Dept_Id	Dname	Prof_Id

If Dept_id is put in professor table this means that the professor with a particular Id manages the department whose id is given by Dept_Id.

Now every professor does not manage a department, so there would be a lot of null values in the dept_id column of the professor table and only those professors who are managing any department will have some values in the dept_id column, the rest will have NULL values.

A database state may look like this:

PROFESSOR

Id	*Fname*	*Lname*	*Salary*	*Dept_Id*
101	Gita	Sharma	10000	10
102	Pawan	Yadav	20000	NULL
103	Preeti	Garg	15000	13
104	Amit	Goyal	10000	NULL
105	Deepa	Aggarwal	30000	NULL
106	Vijay	Pandit	20000	31
107	Arpit	Goyal	15000	NU:LL
108	Pooja	Jain	30000	40

On the other hand if we put the Prof_Id field in the department table, then it says that this particular department with a particular Dept_id and dname is managed by this particular professor whose id is prof_id. So it will not contain NULL values.

This is happening because of the total participation consraint from the department table side and partial participation constraint from the professor table side. Not every professor has to manage a department but a department must be managed by some professor.

So the Correct tables will be like this:

PROFESSOR

Id	Fname	Lname	Salary

DEPARTMENT

Dept_Id	Dname	Prof_Id

Note the Prof_id is the foreign key in department table which references the primar key Id of professor table and captures the relationship manages.

Now let us take the BELONGS relationship. Now either I can put the Dept_id (of DEPARTMENT table) in the professor table or put Id (of PROFESOR table) in department table.

The tables will look like this:

PROFESSOR

Id	Fname	Lname	Salary	Dept_Id

Or

DEPARTMENT

Dept_Id	Dname	Prof_Id	Id

Let us take the Department table. Now each department will have 1 record for it in the department table. And we know a number of professor are working in each department . So the database state may look like this.

DEPARTMENT

Dept_Id	*Dname*	*Prof_Id*	*Id*
10	CSE	101	101, 108, 109, 110
13	IT	104	105, 104, 102
31	EC	103	103, 118, 119, 112
40	ME	106	106, 117, 113, 115, 114

Dept_Id shows the department number, dname give the name of the depatrtment. Prof_Id tells who manages the department and Id tells who all professors belong to that department.

So since it is showing multiple values in the id colunn it is not allowed. Then we will have to decompose the table because we can have only a single value in a single row single column.

Now let us look at the other alternative of taking the Professor table. We put the Dept_id into the professor table. So the Id shows the ID of the professor, the fname and lname show the first nname and last name, the salary shows the salary of the professor and the Dept_Id shows which department he belongs to. So there are no problem of null values or multivalues. So the correct option is that we put dept_id in the in the profesor table.

The multiple values are occuring because of the 1:N cardinality ratio constraint between the PROFESSOR – BELONGS – DEPARTMENT relaionship.

So the correct tables will be

PROFESSOR

Id	Fname	Lname	Salary	Dept_Id

DEPARTMENT

Dept_Id	Dname	Prof_Id

Note Dept_Id is the foreign key in the professor table and captures the relationship BELONGS.

Now let us take the HEADS relationship. It is again 1:N and there is only one entity type so there is no question of putting the key attribute of one entity type's table into another entity type's table. It has to be put in the only one entity type which is given and that is the PROFESSOR entity type in this case. Remember this is a recursive relationship.

So the PROFESSOR table becomes like this:

PROFESSOR

Id	Fname	Lname	Salary	Dept_Id	Head_Id

Note that head_id tells that this particular professor given with ID, Id is headed by this particular professor given by ID head_id. Head_Id is a foreign key which refrences the primary key Id of the PROFESSOR table and captures the relationship HEADS.

A following Database state may look like this:

PROFESSOR

Id	*Fname*	*Lname*	*Salary*	*Dept_Id*	*Head_Id*
101	Gita	Sharma	10000	10	102
102	Pawan	Yadav	20000	13	NULL
103	Preeti	Garg	15000	31	102
104	Amit	Goyal	10000	40	106
105	Deepa	Aggarwal	30000	40	104
106	Vijay	Pandit	20000	40	102

The above table shows that Professor with Id 102 is not headed by anyone. 102 is head of professors 101, 103 and 106. 106 I head of 104 and 104 is head of 105.

Let us take the TEACHES relationship. So this is an M:N relationship. Now if we put the Course_Id attribute in PROFESSOR table, which means this professor teaches these particular courses, so we will get multivalues.

On the other hand if we put the Id (Professor's Id) in the course table, which means this course is taught by these many professors, then again it will have multivalues.

PROFESSOR

Id	*Fname*	*Lname*	*Salary*	*Dept_Id*	*Head_Id*	*Course_Id*
101	Gita	Sharma	10000	10	102	CS401, CS 402, CS 403
102	Pawan	Yadav	20000	13	NULL	IT402 , CS 402 CS 403
103	Preeti	Garg	15000	31	102	EC201, EC202
104	Amit	Goyal	10000	40	106	ME101, ME102, ME103
105	Deepa	Aggarwal	30000	40	104	ME103,ME104, ME102
106	Vijay	Pandit	20000	40	102	ME102, ME101,

OR

COURSE

Course Id	*Cname*	*Prof_Id*
CS401	DAA	101
CS402	DBMS	101,102
CS403	OS	101,102
IT402	ITC	102
EC201	EME	103
EC202	WO	103
ME101	SOM	104,106
ME102	ERE	104,105,106
ME103	FM	104,105
ME104	RO	105

So for an M:N relationship you have to create a new table whose name is the name of the relationship with the key as the key attributes of both entity types forming the key of this new table and any attribute given on the relationship type will be the attribute of this new table.

So our New Table TEACHING lloks like this:

Prof id	*Course id*	*Section*
101	CS401	A
101	CS402	B
101	CS403	A
102	IT402	A
102	CS402	B
102	CS403	C
103	EC201	A
103	EC202	A
104	ME101	B
104	ME102	A
104	ME103	C
105	ME103	D
105	ME104	A
105	ME102	B
106	ME102	A
106	ME101	A

Where the combination of the Prof_Id and Course_Id form the key, because niether the Prof_Id is unique, because one professor teaches many courses an neither the course_id can form the key because one course may be taught by many professors.

As you can see the Prof-Id (say 101)occurs many times (cannot alone become the key). The course_Id ay (CS401) occurs many times cannot alone become the key. So the combination of {Prof_Id,

Course_Id} together is unique and therefore these both attributes form the key.

Let us take STUDIES relationship. It is an M:N relationship. For the same reasons given abovc we will form a new table STUDYING.

STUDYING

Student_id	Course_id	Grade

Now here Student_Id and Course_Id together form the key of the table and which Student got what grade in which particular course is captured.

So Finally our ER Diagram given above is reduced to the folloing set of tables (Relations) with the Primary key underlined for the table.

STUDENT

Student_Id	Stu_Name	Address

STUDENT_PHONES

Student_Id	Phone_No

DEPARTMENT

Dept_Id	Dname	Prof_Id

PROFESSOR

Id	Fname	Lname	Salary	Dept_Id	Head_Id

COURSE

Course_Id	Cname

TEACHING

Prof_id	Course_id	Section

STUDYING

Student_id	Course_id	Grade

2.8 Weak Entity Type

Weak Entity types are those which cannot exist on their own that is they do not have their own Primary Key. Their existence is dependent on the existence of another entity type (main entity type). And the combination of the primary key of the main entity type and one attribute from weak entity type makes the key of the weak entity type.

For example, consider an entity EMPLOYEE in a company.

EMPLOYEE

Empid	Empname	Salary	Address	Designation

He may or may not have dependents (wife or children). So the existence of the entity type DEPENDANTS is dependent on the fact whether that employee exist in the company or not. If suppose the employee leaves the company, then we need not keep the details about his dependants.

Our DEPENDANTS table is like this:

DEPENDANTS

Name	Age	Relation_with_Employee

This is represented in an ER diagram as follows:

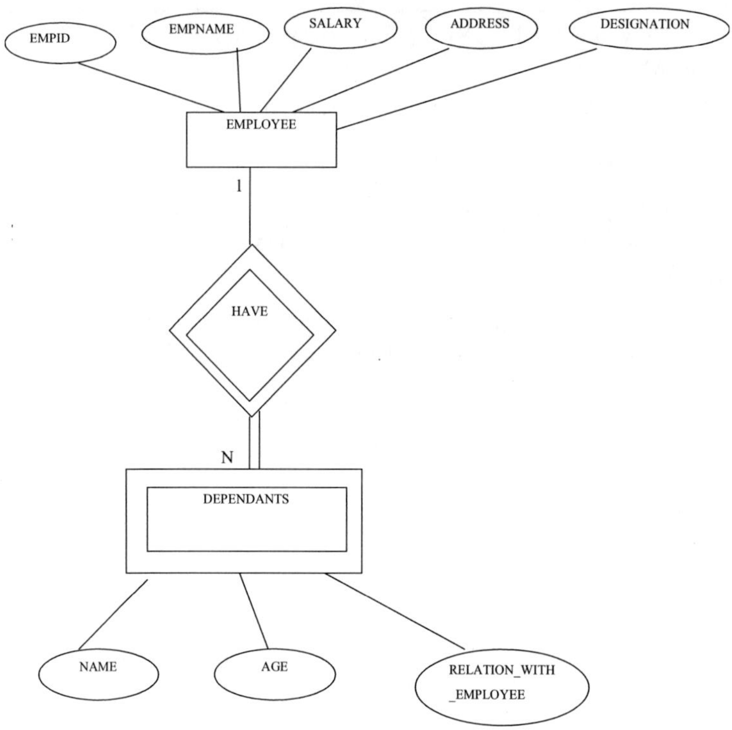

The relationship have is shown by a double Diamond to indicate a weak entity type. The weak entity type DEPANDANT is shown by a double rectangle to indicate weak entity type. An employee may or may not have dependants so partial constraint (shown by single line). The dependants must be of an employee so total constraint shown by double line. An Employee mat have several dependants so 1: N relationship. But the dependant is of a single employee so 1 is on the side of the employee entity type.

When this ER diagram is reduced into tables, then they appear as

EMPLOYEE

Empid	Empname	Salary	Address	Designation

DEPENDANTS

Empid	Name	Age	Relation_with_Employee

Now the EMPLOYEE table has primary key as EmpId and DEPANDANTS table has its primary key as {Empld, Name} together, because it is a weak entity type, cannot have its own primary key.

2.9 Ternary Relationships

Binary relationships are those in which two entity types participate. What we have considered till now in our previous ER diagrams are Binary relationships.

Ternary relationships are those in which three entity type participate. For example, consider example of Relationship with degree = 3.

In which we had which Supplier supplies which part to which project. So it may be shown in an ER diagram as follows:

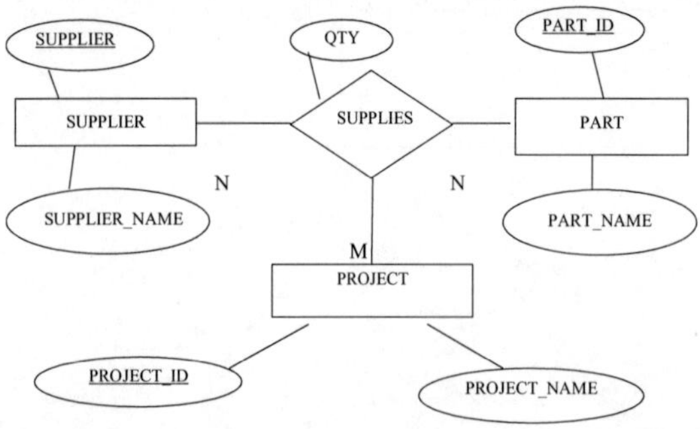

Here 3 entity types participate in the relationship SUPPLIES. When this ER Diagram is reduced to tables it will be as follows.

SUPPLIER

Supplier_Id	Supplier_Name

PART

Part_Id	Part_Name

PROJECT

Project_Id	Project_Name

SUPPLIES

Supplier_Id	Part_Id	Project_Id	Qty

Where the primary key of the SUPPLIES table is the combination of the Primary Keys of all the 3 entity types participating. {Supplier_Id, Part_Id, Project_Id}

Where Supplier_Id is the Primary Key of the Supplier Table

Part_Id is the Primary Key of the Part Table

Project-Id is the primary key of the Project table.

2.10 Subclasses and Superclasses

The STUDENT entity type can further be broken down into different subgroups of students, such as Research Scholar, Post Graduate or an Under Graduate Student. These sub groups are called subclasses and the STUDENT entity type will be called Superclass for each of these subclasses (Research Scholar, Post Graduate, Under Graduate).

2.10.1 Specialization is the process of defining a set of subclasses of an Entity Type. This Entity type is called the Superclass of the specialization.

Why should we make Subclasses.?

The question arises that what is the need to make subclasses, when we can work with a superclass. There are two reasons for this:

(1) A set of attributes may belong to one subclass

(2) A subclass may participate in a Relationship Type.

Let us explain what we mean by the above.

(1) The attributes which are required in all the subclasses will be present in the superclass and they will be inherited by each of the subclasses. The attributes which are specific to a particular subclass will be present in that subclass only.

(2) All subclasses need not participate in all relationship types. If all subclasses need to participate in a relationship type then the superclass will participate in that relationship type. And the subclasses which participate in a specific relationship type will do it seperately, keeping the other subclasses aside.

By the proces of specialization, we can make subclasses of STUDENT entity type.

The new ER diagram may look as follows:

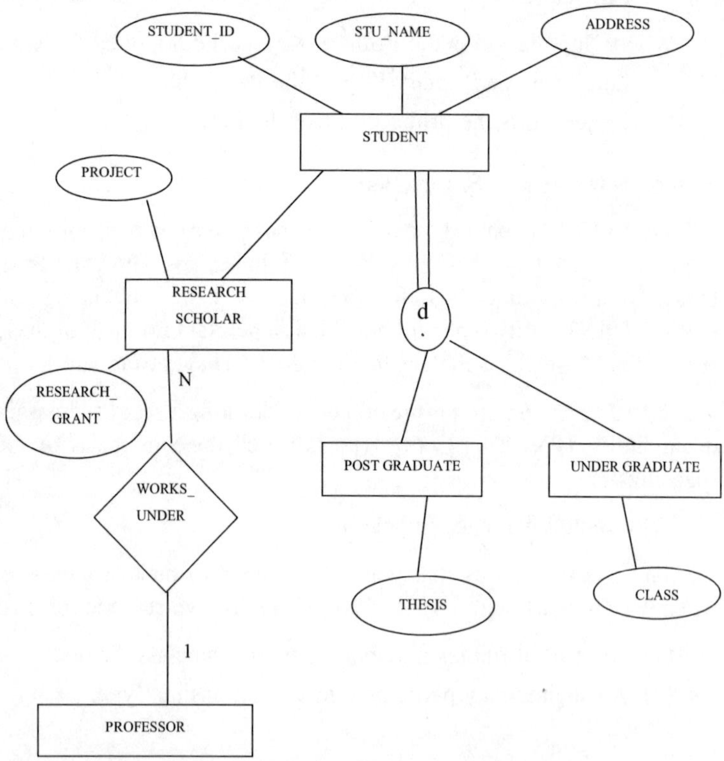

Now the above ER diagram tells us the following facts:

- The STUDENT is a superclass with Student_Id, Student_Name, address as its attributes where student_id is the key and all these 3 attributes are inherited by each of the subclasses.
- The subclasses are Research Scholar, Post Graduate and Under Graduate .
- A Student may or my not be a Research Scholar therefore partial constraint shown by single line.
- A student has to be either a Post Graduate Student or under graduate student therefore total constraint shown by double lines.
- The post graduate student may be doing a thesis and may not belong to a class so it has a specific attribute type thesis.
- The undergraduate student must belong to a class so a specific attribute class.
- The Research Scholar may have specific atributes project and Research_Grant.
- The Research Scholar works under a professor so it participates in a specific relationhip type works_under.
- A professor may have a number of Research Scholar under him so N on the side of Research scholar entity type. A research scholar works under only one professor so 1 on the side of the Professor entity type.

2.10.2 Disjointness

The d sign connecting the post graduate and under graduate entity type indicates the disjointness property. The disjointness property says that either the student belongs to the under graduate subclass or the post graduate subclass but he cannot belong to both of them at the same time.

2.10.3 Generalization

The opposite of Specializtion is generalization. That is to make a superclass from a number of subclasses is known as the process of Generalization.

Suppose we have the following subclasses- full time and part time professors.

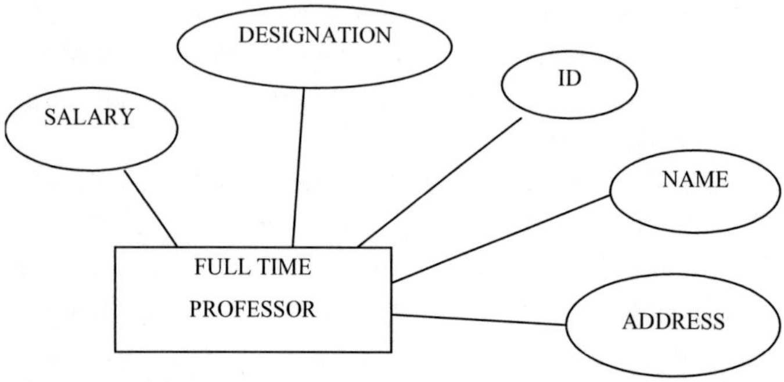

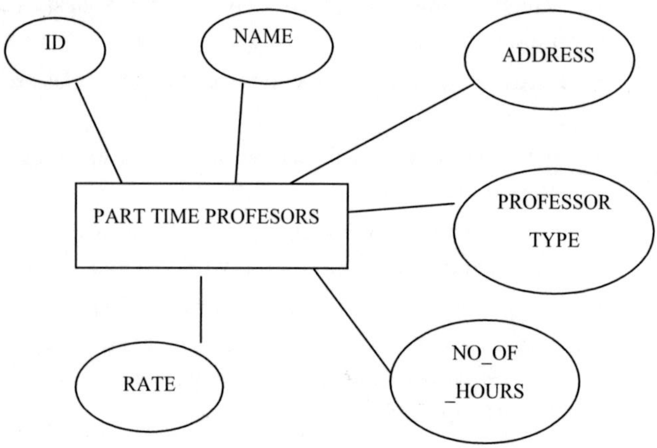

These can be generalized into a superclass PROFESSOR as follows:

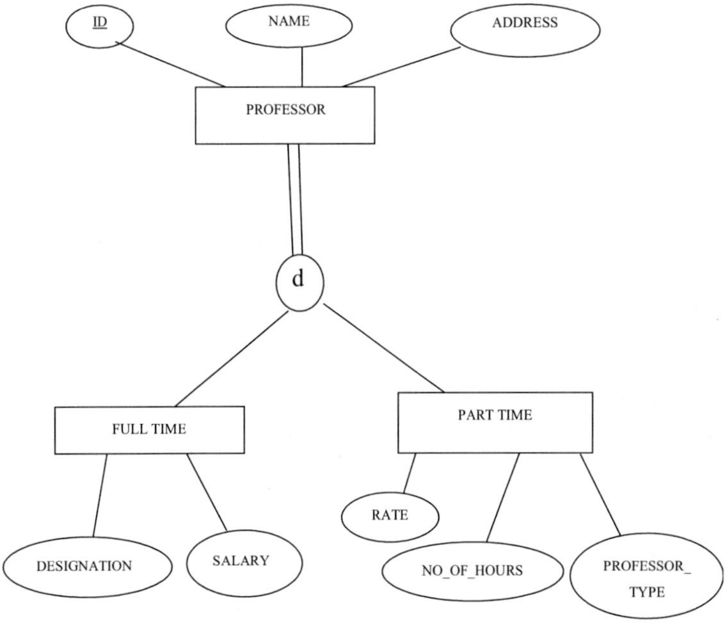

So the common attributes are put in the superclass and the specific attributes have to be put in the subclasses. The disjoint property says that it can either be full time or part time professor but not both at the same time.

2.11 Aggregation

Aggregation is used when we have to define relationship among relationships. In an ER diagram we cannot simply have a relationship with another relationship.

We make an aggregate class first and then define a relationship with that aggregate class. Our aggregate class is composed of 2 entity types with a relationship between them . Now this Aggregate class is to be related with another relationship to indicate a relationship with another relationship.

Let us take an example to explain this.

Suppose we have a manufacturer who makes a deal with a distributor. So it is shown as below:

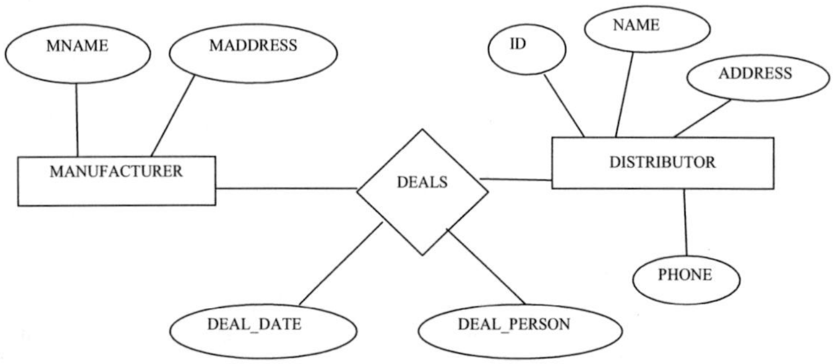

Now if this deal results in supplying a product. Then there exists a relationship among a relationship as follows:

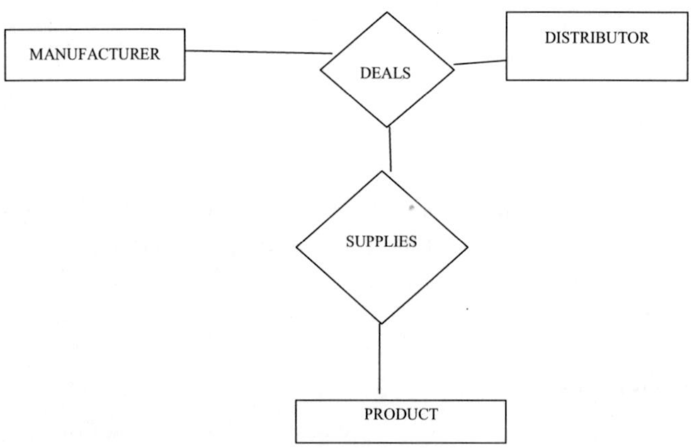

So this is not allowed in an ER diagram to have a relationship with another relationship.

If we make a ternary relationship between manufacturer, distributor and product with deals as the relationship type between them. Then that is equivalent to saying that every deal must supply a product, which might not be the case. Because every deal may not result in supplying a product. Some deals will result in supplying a product others will not.

So to do it properly we will have to make an aggregate class and then the relationship will exist between the aggregate class as follows:

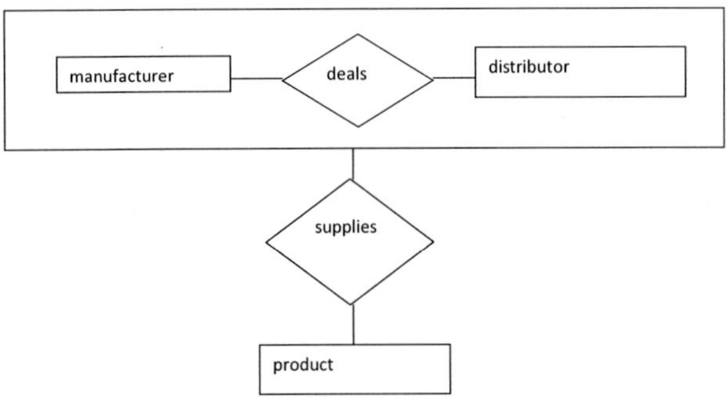

Now the aggregate class is higher level abstract object. To make it into an Extended Entity Relationship Model (EER Model), we will have to make the deals relationship a weak entity type which will be shown as follows:

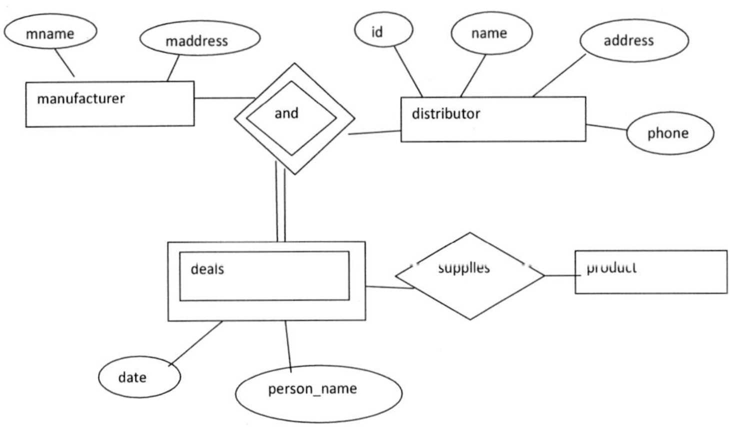

Chapter - 3

Relational Model and Relational Algebra

3.1 Introduction

In a relational model, the database is represented as a collection of Relations. And Relations are nothing but what we commonly call tables.

The Relation is in the form of a table which has values in each row and each column. Each row has a collection of values which are related. In informal terms it may be treated as a record of a particular person (for an employee table) or of a particular student (for a student table) etc.

In the relational model, a particular row in a particular table represents the values of a real world entity or a relationship.

The name of the table and the names of the column are used to identify the meaning of the values given in each row.

Let us take an example.

The student table (or Relation) would represent the facts about a particular student entity. The column names Student_id, Student_name, address tell us what data is placed in these columns and how we should interpret it.

The data values placed in each row based on the column each value is in are all of the same type representing the column type.

For example, student_id is a column, all the values of this column in each row would be digits (because they cannot have alphabets or special characters) and we give this type when we create the table.

Similarly the student name would have only alphabets (it cannot have digits or special characters) whereas address would be of type alphanumeric (where we can have alphabets, digits as well as special characters).

In a formal relational model, a row is called a tuple, a column name is known as an attribute and each table name is a Relation. The datatype of a column i.e. the type of values that can appear in each column is called a domain.

3.2 Domains, Attributes, Tuples and Relations

A domain D is a set of atomic values. By atomic we mean that each value in the domain cannot be divided further as far as the relational model is concerned.

For example, phone number is a 10 digit number which is indivisible and the domain is a set of digits containing 10 digits.

Another attribute age should vary between 18 and 80. So the domain will be 18 to 80. We cannot have a 2 year old child working or a 100 year old person working. So the domain decides the range of values that you can choose from.

Another attribute department codes can be from { CSE, EC, IT, MCA, EE } etc. Here a particular set of codes are given from which you have to choose only. These can be the enumerated types of data.

Mathematically, a relation is defined as a set of tuples. The tuples may be in any order, there is no particular order for this set.

Values in the tuple must be atomic that is they cannot be divided further. No composite or multivalued attributes are allowed. To represent multivalued attributes, we need to make another relation for them and composite attributes are represented only by their simple component attributes.

Relational Model Notations:

(1) A relational schema R is denoted by R(A1, A2 ....An) where A1, A2, ...An are attributes of the relation R.

(2) An n –tuple t in a relation r(R) is denoted by t = < v1, v2 .... Vn> where vi is the value corresponding to attribute Ai.

t[Ai] refers to the value vi in tuple t for attribute Ai.

3.3 Relational Constraints and Relational database Schemas

There are some restrictions that are put on the data of a relational database and they are known as Relational Constraints. There are four types of constraints and they are known as

(1) Domain Constraint
(2) Key Constraint
(3) Entity Integrity Constraint
(4) Referential integrity Constraint

Let us describe each one in detail.

(1) Domain Constraint: The Domain Constraint specify that the value of each attribute A must be an atomic value from the domain dom(A).

The data types associated with the domains include integer where only numbers are allowed, real –numbers where decimals are allowed, characters where A-Z characters are allowed or integers or special characters are allowed. These can be char which are fixed length strings or varchar which can be variable length strings.

The data types can also be of type date, time or timestamps or can be enumerated types where values can be picked from only some possible values which are already given in a set, example departments [CSE, IT, MCA, EE, EC} etc.

(2) Key Constraints or constraints on null: A relation may be defined as a set of tuples. The tuples have to be different from each other. No two tuples can have all the values same of their attributes – because this in other words is known as duplicate data. They must differ at least on one attribute, which is normally the key, because the key is unique for each tuple. No two tuples can have the same key otherwise the definition of key is violated, because key has to be unique.

Formally it can be stated as no two tuples can have the same superkey which can be denoted as

$$t1[SK] = t2[SK\}$$

As we know that the key is the minimal superkey that is if we remove any attribute from the key (if key is made up of 2 or more attributes). Then the new key K' is not a super key any more.

If there is one attribute which makes up the key then that cannot be removed. The value of a key attribute can be used to identify uniquely each tuple in the relation.

Example,

empid is the key.

empid, empname, is a superkey

empid, empname, Date_of_Birth is a superkey

In general, a relation may have more than one key. In such a case, each of the keys is called a candidate key.

For example, a relation Employee may have empid as a key and also aadhar-no can also be a key. Similarly for a Vehicle, a License_ plate_number can be a key and engine_serial_ number can also become the key.

(3) Entity Integrity Constraint: The meaning of entity integrity lies in the fact that how can you maintain the integrity of an entity. An entity is determined by its primary key attribute. The primary key attribute is the one which uniquely identifies an entity and therefore the entity is known by its primary key attribute. So the Entity Integrity Constraint specifies that the primary key attribute should not be NULL because if that is NULL, the entity cannot be identified and there is no means to get all other attributes of that entity.

(4) Referential Integrity Constraint: In Referential Integrity Constraint, there are 2 relations in the context, one is the referencing relation and one is the referenced relation. There are 2 keys involved, one is the primary key and the other is the foreign key.

The foreign key belongs to the referencing relation and the primary key belongs to the referenced relation. Basically the foreign key of the referencing relation refers to the primary key of the referenced relation.

For Example, In our database we have the following tables:

COURSE

CourseName	CourseID

STUDENT

StudentID	StudentName	Address

STUDENT_PHONES

Student_ID	Phone_No

DEPARTMENT

Dname	DeptID	Prof_ID

PROFESSOR

id	Fname	Lname	Dept_ID	Salary	Head_ID

TEACHING

Prof_ID	Course_ID	Section

STUDYING

Course_ID	Student_ID	Grade

Now let us identify the primary keys of each table.

The primary key of COURSE table is COURSEID

The primary key of STUDENT table is STUDENTID

The primary key of DEPARTMENT table is DEPTID

The primary key of PROFESSOR table is ID

The primary key of TEACHING table is {PROF_ID, COURSE_ID}

The primary key of STUDYING table is {STUDENT_ID, COURSE_ID}

The primary key of STUDENT_PHONES table is {STUDENT_ID, PHONE_NO}

Let us now see the foreign keys in each table and to which primary key they refer to.

Foreign Key DEPT_ID of PROFESSOR table refers to primary key of DEPARTMENT table DEPTID

Foreign Key HEAD_ID of PROFESSOR table refers to
primary key of PROFESSOR table ID

Foreign Key PROF_ID of TEACHING table refers to
primary key of PROFESSOR table ID

Foreign Key COURSE_ID of TEACHING table refers to
primary key of COURSE table COURSEID

Foreign Key COURSE_ID of STUDYING table refers to
primary key of COURSE table COURSEID

Foreign Key STUDENT_ID of STUDYING table refers to
primary key of STUDENT table STUDENTID

Foreign Key STUDENT_ID of STUDENT_PHONES table refers to
primary key of STUDENT table STUDENTID

Foreign Key PROF_ID of DEPARTMENT table refers to
primary key of PROFESSOR table ID

Remember the TEACHING table does not have a primary key of its own. Both the foreign keys combined together form the primary key of the TEACHING table i.e. (PROF_ID, COURSE_ID). It indicates which professor teaches which course uniquely since there may be more than one professor teaching a single course and one professor may teach many courses.

Similarly the STUDYING table does not have a primary key of its own, both the foreign keys combined together form the primary key of the STUDYING table i.e. (COURSE_ID, STUDENT_ID). It indicates which student studies in which course uniquely since there may be a student who studies more than one course and one course may be studied by more than one student.

Now the Referential Integrity Constraint says that if we have a value in the foreign key attribute of the referencing table, then the corresponding value must exist in the primary key attribute of the referenced table.

It should not be the case that a value is existing in the foreign key attribute, but no record is present of that value in the primary key attribute.

For Example,

If I have a value of 5 in DEPT_ID field of PROFESSOR table, then a record with a value of 5 should exist in the DEPTID field of the DEPARTMENT table and it should not be the case that the DEPARTMENT table has no record with a value of 5 in the DEPTID field.

3.4 Relational Algebra Operations

There are a number of operations which are used to manipulate the data.

A relational model uses two types of operations to manipulate the data and both of these types make up the relational algebra operations.

These two types are:

(1) Set Theoretic Operations

(2) Operations specially designed for relational algebra.

The set theoretic operations are taken from the set theory of mathematics because the Relation or tables are defined as a set of tuples, so therefore the set theory operations can be applied on them.

Set theoretic operations are of four types:

(1) Union

(2) Intersection

(3) Set Difference

(4) Cartesian product

Operations specially designed for database are of 3 types:

(1) Select

(2) Project

(3) Join

Let us describe each one in detail.

3.4.1 The Set Theoretic Operations

The set operations Union, Intersection and Set difference are used to merge the elements of two sets in different ways.

These can be applied to the relational database where two different relations are used in place of two sets.

The three set operations Union, Intersection and Set Difference require that the type of tuples of two relations must be same. By same we mean that they must be union compatible.

Union Compatibility: This is the condition where two relations must have the same number of attributes and each pair of corresponding attributes must be from the same domain.

To explain the above. Let us take some examples:

(1) ***Union Operation***: As you know, when we say A U B, then the result contains all rows from the relation A and all rows from the relation B and duplicate rows are deleted.

Now consider a relation A as follows:

Student_Id	***Student_Name***	***Address***
101	Alka	Delhi
102	Sita	Bombay
103	Gita	Madras

Now consider a relation B as follows:

Student_Id	***Student_Name***	***Address***
104	Pawan	Poona
105	Amit	Bombay
102	Sita	Bombay

When we do union of relation A and relation B as A U B, we get the relation as follows:

Student_Id	***Student_Name***	***Address***
101	Alka	Delhi
102	Sita	Bombay
103	Gita	Madras
104	Pawan	Poona
105	Amit	Bombay

Here the student with student_id 102 was present in both relations A and B, so it was duplicate and hence was put only once in the resultant table.

Now here we see that the two tables A and B are union compatible, that is they have the same number of attributes (i.e. student_id, Student_name, address) and the student-id, Student_name and address are from the same domain (i.e. student_id contains only digits, student_name and address contains only characters).

Now let us consider two relations P and Q as follows:

P

Student_Id	*Student_Name*	*Address*
101	Alka	Delhi
102	Sita	Bombay
103	Gita	Madras

Q

Student_Id	*Student_Name*
104	Pawan
105	Amit

Now they are not union compatible, because table or relation P has 3 attributes and table Q has 2 attributes and if we take union of P and Q, then we will not get proper relation with all rows having equal number of columns so therefore we cannot take union of the tables P and Q.

Consider another set of tables X and Y

X

Student_Id	*Student_Name*	*Address*
101	Alka	Delhi
102	Sita	Bombay
103	Gita	Madras

Y

Student_Id	***Student_Name***	***Date_of_Birth***
104	Pawan	12-JUL-1988
105	Amit	14-MAR-1986
106	Preeti	11-APR-1987

Now here X has 3 attributes and Y also has 3 attributes, but their domain are different. Student_Id and student_Name have the same domain, that is they pick up values from digits and characters respectively but the column address and date_of_birth is different. Address picks up values from char whereas date_of_birth is of type date. Therefore they are not union compatible because domains are different therefore we will not get a proper table if we do X union of Y,, because columns must have the same type of values.

(2) Intersection Operation: This is represented by $A \cap B$ which gives the values which are common in both tables A and B.

Let us Consider A and B as follows:

A

Student_Id	***Student_Name***	***Address***
101	Alka	Delhi
102	Sita	Bombay
103	Gita	Madras

B

Student_Id	***Student_Name***	***Address***
104	Pawan	Poona
105	Amit	Bombay
102	Sita	Bombay

So $A \cap B$ gives

Student_Id	***Student_Name***	***Address***
102	Sita	Bombay

That is rows or tuples which are common in A and B, which was only one row 102 that is why that is in the resultant table.

(3) Set Difference Operation: This is represented by A – B, consider the same tables A and B again,

So A –B gives

Student_Id	***Student_Name***	***Address***
101	Alka	Delhi
103	Gita	Madras

The resultant table gives values containing in A, with any common values eliminated and no value from table B is also included in the resultant table.

Now for the same reasons given above in the Union Operation, the Intersection Operation and the Set Difference operation require themselves to have the union compatibility property otherwise they will not get the correct answers in the resultant tables.

(4) Cartesian Product Operation: This is represented by A x B. In Cartesian Product, the Union Compatibility condition is not required because we would be multiplying each row of 1st relation with each row of 2nd relation and the number of attributes may be different in both relations. The resultant relation would have the combined sum of number of attributes of both relations.

To put it more formally, consider the relation A (A1, A2, …..An) and B (B1, B2 …..Bm). then the resultant relation will have n+m attributes. And if relation A contains Na number of rows and relation B contains Nb number of rows, then A x B will contain Na * Nb number of rows, where A x B represents the Cartesian Product of A and B.

Suppose we have two tables A and B as follows:

A

Student_Id	***Student_Name***	***Address***
101	Sita	Delhi
102	Gita	Bombay
103	Pawan	Madras
104	Preeti	Poona

B

Dept_Name	*Date_of_Birth*
CSE	12-JUL-1988
IT	14-MAR-1986
MCA	11-APR-1987

The table A has 3 attributes (n) and 4 rows (Na). The table B has 2 attributes (m) and 3 rows (Nb).

The resultant table A x B (Cartesian Product) will have n + m (3 + 2 = 5) number of attributes and Na * Nb (4 * 3 = 12) rows as follows:

Student_Id	*Student_Name*	*Address*	*Dept_Name*	*Date_of_Birth*
101	Sita	Delhi	CSE	12-JUL-1988
101	Sita	Delhi	IT	14-MAR-1986
101	Sita	Delhi	MCA	11-APR-1987
102	Gita	Bombay	CSE	12-JUL-1988
102	Gita	Bombay	IT	14-MAR-1986
102	Gita	Bombay	MCA	11-APR-1987
103	Pawan	Madras	CSE	12-JUL-1988
103	Pawan	Madras	IT	14-MAR-1986
103	Pawan	Madras	MCA	11-APR-1987
104	Preeti	Poona	CSE	12-JUL-1988
104	Preeti	Poona	IT	14-MAR-1986
104	Preeti	Poona	MCA	11-APR-1987

3.5 Operations Particularly Designed for the Relational Database

There are 3 operations which are particularly designed for the relational database.

(1) Select

(2) Project

(3) Join

Let us describe each one in detail.

(1) The Select Operation: This is denoted by the symbol σ in the relational algebra. The select operation is used to select some rows based on some condition.

For example, suppose in the STUDENT table. I want a record of the student whose student_id is 101.

So I will give the expression in Relational Algebra as

$$\text{Result} \leftarrow \sigma_{\text{Student\_id} = \text{'101'}} (\text{STUDENT})$$

Where STUDENT is the relation from which you need to access the information and student_id = '101'is the condition.

If you have the following STUDENT table

STUDENT

Student_Id	***Student_Name***	***Address***
101	Sita	Delhi
102	Gita	Bombay
103	Pawan	Madras
104	Preeti	Poona

Then the RESULT table will be

RESULT

Student_Id	***Student_Name***	***Address***
101	Sita	Delhi

(2) The Project Operation: This is denoted by the symbol ∏ in relational Algebra. Just as the select operation is used to select some rows, the project operation is used to select a particular column.

Let us consider our STUDENT table again.

$$\text{Result} \leftarrow \Pi_{\text{Address}} (\text{STUDENT})$$

So we get the address column in the RESULT table.

RESULT

Address
Delhi
Bombay
Madras
Poona

Now let us take an example to see how the Select and the project operations can be used together.

Suppose our query is to retrieve the Student_Id and Student_Name of students who live in Bombay.

Our STUDENT table is as follows:

STUDENT

Student_Id	*Student_Name*	*Address*
101	Alka	Delhi
102	Sita	Bombay
103	Gita	Madras
104	Pawan	Poona
105	Amit	Bombay

Result <- $\Pi_{\text{Student\_id,Student\_Name}}(\sigma_{\text{Address = 'Bombay'}}$ (STUDENT))

RESULT

Student_Id	*Student_Name*
102	Sita
105	Amit

(3) Join Operation: This is denoted by the symbol $\bowtie$.

The Join Operation is used to combine related tuples from two different relations into single tuples.

Consider our two tables Department and Professor.

DEPARTMENT(Dname, Dept_Id)

PROFESSOR(Id, Name, Dept_Id, Salary, Head_Id)

Now we need to find out the Name, Id of the Professors and the Names of the departments they work in.

Dept_Prof<- DEPARTMENT $\bowtie_{\text{Department.Dept\_Id = Professor. Dept\_Id}}$ PROFESSOR

Result < - $\Pi_{\text{Id, Name, Dname}}$(Dept_Prof)

Here Dept_Id in PROFESSOR table is the foreign key and Dept_Id in the DEPARTMENT table is the primary key. So this refers to the referential integrity constraint.

Suppose we have the following tables of DEPARTMENT and PROFESSOR.

DEPARTMENT

Dname	*Dept_Id*
CSE	10
IT	13
EC	31
MCA	50
ME	40
EE	12

PROFESSOR

Id	*Name*	*Dept_Id*	*Salary*	*Head_Id*
101	Sita	10	10000	NULL
102	Gita	10	20000	101
103	Pawan	13	30000	110
104	Preeti	13	40000	103
105	Deepa	31	10000	110
106	Amit	50	20000	110
107	Anjana	40	30000	110
108	Nisha	12	40000	110
109	Nikhil	12	20000	108
110	Nidhi	13	30000	103

Now the join will join the values where the dept_id of DEPARTMENT table matches the Dept_Id of PROFESSOR table. And it will not give us the Cartesian product but just those rows which match.

So the Result Table will be

RESULT

Id	*Name*	*Dname*
101	Sita	CSE
102	Gita	CSE
103	Pawan	IT
104	Preeti	IT
105	Deepa	EC
106	Amit	MCA
107	Anjana	ME
108	Nisha	EE
109	Nikhil	EE
110	Nidhi	IT

Let us use the Select, Project and Join together in a query.

Consider the following Tables

PROFESSOR(Id, Name, Dept_Id, Salary, Head_Id)

TEACHING(Prof_Id, Course_Id)

Query: Retrieve the name and salary of all the professors who are teaching the course_id 'CS402'.

$$PROF \leftarrow \sigma_{Course\_id = 'CS402'} (TEACHING)$$

$$R1 \leftarrow PROFESSOR \bowtie_{Id = Prof\_Id} PROF$$

$$RESULT \leftarrow \Pi_{Name,\ Salary}(R1)$$

Let us take examples of Union, Intersection and Set Difference and then we will describe the division operation and the aggregate functions.

Example – Union Operation

Query: Select the student names who study Course_Id 'CS401' or Course_Id 'CS402' or both.

Consider the tables

STUDENT(Student_Id, Student_Name, Address)

STUDYING(Course_Id, Student_Id, Grade)

$$R1 <- \sigma_{\text{Course\_id = 'CS401'}} (\text{STUDYING})$$

$$R2 <- \sigma_{\text{Course\_id = 'CS402'}} (\text{STUDYING})$$

$$R3 <- \Pi_{\text{Student\_Name}} (R1 \underset{\text{Student\_Id = Student\_Id}}{\bowtie} \text{STUDENT})$$

$$R4 <- \Pi_{\text{Student\_Name}} (R2 \underset{\text{Student\_Id = Student\_Id}}{\bowtie} \text{STUDENT})$$

$$\text{Result} <- R3 \cup R4$$

Example – Intersect Operation

Query: Select the student names who study Course_Id 'CS401' and Course_Id 'CS402' both together.

Consider the tables

STUDENT(Student_Id, Student_Name, Address)

STUDYING(Course_Id, Student_Id, Grade)

$$R1 <- \sigma_{\text{Course\_id = 'CS401'}} (\text{STUDYING})$$

$$R2 <- \sigma_{\text{Course\_id = 'CS402'}} (\text{STUDYING})$$

$$R3 <- \Pi_{\text{Student\_Name}} (R1 \underset{\text{Student\_Id = Student\_Id}}{\bowtie} \text{STUDENT})$$

$$R4 <- \Pi_{\text{Student\_Name}} (R2 \underset{\text{Student\_Id = Student\_Id}}{\bowtie} \text{STUDENT})$$

$$\text{Result} <- R3 \cap R4$$

Example – Set Difference Operation

Query: Select the student names who do not study Course_Id 'CS401'.

$$ALL\_STUDENTS <- \Pi_{Student\_Id}(STUDENT)$$

$$STUD\_WITH\_CS401 <- \Pi_{Student\_Id}(\sigma_{Course\_id = 'CS401'}(STUDYING))$$

$$R2 <- \Pi_{Student\_Id}(ALL\_STUDENTS - STUD\_WITH\_CS401)$$

$$Result <- \Pi_{Student\_Name}(R2 \bowtie_{Student\_Id = Student\_Id} STUDENT)$$

3.6 The Division Operation

Division is applied to two functions. Suppose we need to find out the names of all students who study all the courses that the student with student id = 1009013001 studies.

Let us first take general tables A and B and then we will take the example of the student table and show the answer of the above query.

The division operation is denoted by the sign÷ .

We divide table A with table B and it gives us the table C.

We say C (Y) = A (Z) ÷ .B(X)

Let X be the attributes of table B

And Z be the attributes of table A

Then Y = Z – X

Y will be the attributes representing the attributes of Z minus the Attributes of X.

Suppose there is a relation A with attributes (P, Q).

There is a relation B with attributes (Q)

Then C = A ÷ B will have attribute P only.

Because here Z = (P, Q)
X = Q

And Y = Z – X
= (P, Q) – (Q)
= P

Suppose our relation A has the following table.

A

P	Q
P1	Q1
P1	Q2
P1	Q3
P2	Q1
P2	Q2
P3	Q1
P3	Q2
P3	Q3
P3	Q4
P4	Q1
P4	Q3

B

Q
Q1
Q2
Q3

Now the division operation says that if we have A ÷ B, then the values of attributes of A should occur with all the values of attributes of B.

Now b has an attribute Q which has values Q1, Q2 and Q3.

The values of A has P1 which exists with all the 3 values of Q of table B. Q1, Q2 and Q3.

Now consider P2, P2 occurs with only 2 values of Q of B and those are Q1 and Q2 and does not occur with Q3 . Therefore P2 is not divided by B.

Now consider P3, P3 occurs with Q1, Q2, Q3 and Q4. Our requirement was that it should occur with Q1, Q2 and Q3, If it occurs with an extra Q4 then it does not matter since it satisfies our condition that it occurs with Q1, Q2 and Q3. Therefore p3 is also selected

Now look at P4, it occurs with Q1 and Q3 and it does not occur with Q2. So it is not selected. So therefore our C table will consist of P1 and P3.

C

P
P1
P3

Also the C table has attributes Y where Y = Z – X .

Here Z that is table A was having attributes P and Q.. B table was having attributes Q. So the C table has attributes P.

Which is Z – X = (P, Q – Q) = P

Now let us go back to our example of STUDENT table.

STUDENT (student_id, Student_name, address)
STUDYING(course_id, student_id, grade)

Now we need to find out the names of all students who study all the courses that the student with student-id = '1009013001' studies.

So first we need to find out the courses that the student with student-id = '1009013001' studies.

COURSES-OF-STUD-WITH-ROLLNO <- Π_{Course_Id} ($\sigma_{Student\_id\ =\ '1009013001'}$ (STUDYING))

Then we need to find out the combinations of students (or student ids) which occurs with all the courses that are studied by the student _id = 1009013001.

From the studying table we need all the student_ids with course-ids.

ALL-STUDENTS <- $\Pi_{Student\_Id,\ Course\_id}$(STUDYING)

Now we need to divide the ALL-STUDENTS withCOURSES-OF-STUD-WITH-ROLLNO.

R1< - ALL-STUDENTS ÷ COURSES-OF-STUD-WITH-ROLLNO.

Remember ALL-STUDENTS has attributes Student-Id and Course_id and COURSES-OF-STUD-WITH-ROLLNO. Has attribute course_id.

So after the division R1 has only attribute student_id.,

Here Z = Student-id, Course_id

X = Course_id

So Z – X = Student_id.

Now we need to join R1 with the student table to find out the names of the students, because R1 contains those students which study all the courses that the student with student-id = 1009013001 studies.

Result <- $\Pi_{\text{Student\_Name}}$ (R1 $\bowtie_{\text{Student\_Id = Student\_Id}}$ STUDENT)

3.7 Aggregate Functions

The aggregate functions are:

(1) Count

(2) Sum

(3) Avg

(4) Min

(5) Max

Let us use a query to explain each in relational Algebra.

(1) Count the total number of students in the database.

R(NO-OF-STUDENT) < - $\delta_{\text{Count(Student-id)}}$ (STUDENT)

We use the d operator for aggregate funcgions. The result is in the new table R, we need to give it a column name. We give in the brackets the No-of-student.

So if you want to use the count of the total number of students, you can use the attribute no-of-student in further queries if required.

(2) Find the sum of the salaries of all professors.

R(TOTAL-SALARY) < - $\delta_{\text{Sum(SALARY)}}$ (professor)

Now the sum of the salaries of all professors are stored in the total-salary column of the R table.

(3) Find the Max, Min and Avg salary of all professors.

R(MAX-SALARY) < - $\delta_{MAX(SALARY)}$ (professor)

R(MIN-SALARY) < - $\delta_{MIN(SALARY)}$ (professor)

R(AVG-SALARY) < - $\delta_{AVG(SALARY)}$ (professor)

The GROUP BY clause can also be used in the aggregate functions.

Query: Find the Avg salaries of professors of each department.

R (Dept-no, Avg-salary)< - Dept_id$\delta_{AVG(SALARY)}$ (professor)

Now in this case, each dept-id along with the average salaries of all the professors in that department will be listed. The department ids will exist in the table R under the column name dept_no and the average salaries will exist under the column name Avg-salary

3.8 The Tuple Relational Calculus

The difference between Relational Calculus and Relational Algebra is that Relational Algebra through the series of queries tells us how to retrieve. Whereas Relational calculus put its focus on what to retrieve.

In a Relational Calculus there are tuple variables and their range relations.

3.8.1 Tuple Variables

Relational Calculus defines a number of tuple variables. Normally each tuple variable has a range to deal with. This range is the database relation on which the tuple variable is specified. So the values are taken fro any one tuple of the database relation.

Let us take n example to demonstrate.

A simple Relational Calculus query can be given as follows:

{t | COND (t)}

Where t represents a tuple variable and COND (t) represents a conditional expression which will be used over t.

The result of the query is the set of all tuples t which will satisfy the condition given by COND(t).

Example Query: Find all Professors whose salary is greater than Rs. 20000.

This can be expressed as follows in the tuple calculus expression.

{ t | PROFESSOR (t) and t.Salary > 20000 }

Here the condition is specified by two expressions PROFESSOR(t) and t.Salary > 20000.

The expression PROFESSOR (t) specifies that the range of the relation of tuple variable t is PROFESSOR.

The expression t.Salary > 20000 says that in the table PROFESSOR wherever we get salary matching over 20000, that tuple will be retrieved.

Where t.salary represents the attribute salary of tuple variable t.

If we want to retrieve some attributes we may give as follows:

{t.Id, t.fname, t.lname | PROFESSOR(t) and t.Salary > 20000}

Now this will not retrieve the whole tuple but only two attributes that match the condition.

So in order to sum up the tuple calculus expression requires the following:

(1) For each tuple variable t, the range relation R. This is depicted as R(t).

(2) A condition to select the tuples. Only those tuple for which the condition evaluates to TRUE will be selected.

(3) A set of attribute that you want to retrieve.

Let us take a query where we use all the above mentioned parameters.

Query: Retrieve the name and salary of the Professor whose Id is '101'.

{t.fname, t.lname, t.salary | PROFESSOR (t) AND t.Id = '101'}

3.8.2 Formulas in Tuple Relational Calculus

A general expression is of the form

{t1.Ai, t2.Aj, t3.Ak .....tn.Am | COND (t1, t2 .....tn, tn+1, tn+2 ....tn+m) }

Where t1, t2 .....tn, tn+1, tn+2 ......tn+m are tuple variables.

Ai is the atribute of the Relation on which ti Ranges.

COND is a condition or a formula.

A formula is made of atoms.

There can be following types of atoms:

(1) R(ti)

where R is Relation Name and ti Tuple Variable which ranges over R.

(2) ti.A operator tj.B

where operator is any operator of the form { =, <, < =, >, >=, ≠ }

ti and tj are tuple variables. A is the attribte of the relation on which ti ranges and B is the attribute of the relation on which tj ranges.

(3) C operator ti.A

Where operator is from the set { =, <, < =, >, >=, ≠ }

ti is a tuple variables. A is the attribte of the relation on which ti ranges and C a constant value.

A formula (condition) is made up of one or more atoms which are connected via the logical operators AND, OR an NOT.

The formulas may be given as follows:

(1) Every atom is a formula

(2) If F1 and F2 are formulas, then the following are also formulas:

(a) (F1 AND F2)

(b) (F1 OR F2)

(c) NOT (F1)

(d) NOT F2

The truth values are given as follows:

(a) (F1 AND F2) is TRUE if both F1 and F2 are TRUE otherwise it is FALSE

(b) (F1 OR F2) is FALSE if both F1 AND F2 are FALSE otherwise it is TRUE.

(c) NOT (F1) is TRUE if F1 is FALSE. It is FALSE if F1 is TRUE.

(d) NOT (F2) is TRUE if F2 is FALSE. It is FALSE if F2 is TRUE.

3.8.3 Existential and Universal Quantifiers

Two special symbols called quantifiers appear in formulas, they are as follows:

(1) Universal Quantifier (¥) and

(2) Existential Quantifier (э)

A tuple variable is said to be bound if it is quantified (that is appears with ¥ or э).

A tuple variable is said to be free if it exists without the quantifier (¥ or э).

For Example, consider the following formulas:

F1: D.Dname = 'IT'

F2: (э P) (D.Dept_id = P.Dept_id)

F3: (¥ D) D.head_id = '101'

Now in formula F1, D is free because it is not quantified.

In F2 D is free and P is bound because P is quantified.

In F3 D is bound because it is quantified.

Rules for Formulas

If it is given a formula as (эt) (F) where t is a tuple variable, then the formula (¥ t) (F) evaluates to TRUE if there exists at least one tuple in which F evaluaes to TRUE.

If it is given a formula as (¥ t) (F) where t is a tuple variable, then the formula (¥ t) (F) evaluates to TRUE if there exists all (every tuple) in which F evaluaes to TRUE.

Example Queries using Existential Quantifiers

Q1. Retrieve the name and salary of all Professors who work in 'IT' Department.

{ t.fname, t.lname t.salary | PROFESSOR (t) AND (ɘ d) (DEPARTMENT (d) AND d.dname = 'IT' AND d.Dept_id = t.Dept_id) }

Q2. For each Professor, rerieve the professor's first name and last name and the first name and last name of his head.

{ p.fname, p.lname h.fname, h.lname | (PROFESSOR (p) and PROFESSOR (h) AND p.head_id = h.Id) }

3.9 The Domain Relational Calculus

The Domain Relational Calculus is also like Tuple Relational Calculus. The difference lies in the fact that in Tuple Relational Calculus we have the relation over which the tuple ranges. And in Domain Relational Calculus, we will have individual attributes which will range over the individual domains insead of tuples.

An expression of the Domain Calculus is of he form:

{x1, x2 ...xn | COND (x1, x2 ....xn, xn + 1, xn+2 ...x n+ m) }

Where x1, x2, ...xn are domain variables that range over domains of attributes and COND is a condition or formula of the Domain Relational Calculus.

The atoms of a Domain Relational Calculus is a little different from that of the Tuple Relational Calculus.

The atoms may be as follows:

(1) If there is a Relation R (x1, x2, ...xj) where R is the name of the relation and xi whee 1 <= i < = j is the Domain Variable, then there must exist a tuple in the relation where xi is the ith attribute value of the tuple.

{ x1, x2, ...xn | R (x1 x2 x3) AND ...... }

(2) An Atom may be of a form xi operator xj where operator is one of the comparison operators in the set { =, <, < =, >, >=, ≠} and xi and xj are Domain Variables.

(3) An atom my be of the form xi operator C or C operator xj where operator is one of the comparison operators in the set { =, <, < =, >, >=, ≠ } and xi and xj are Domain Variables and C is a constant value.

Example Queries

Q1. Retrieve the Id and Salary of all professors whose first name = 'Ajay' and last name = 'Bhatia' .

The Professor table is as follows

Id	fname	lname	Salary	Dept_Id	Head_Id

Where Id = a
Fname = b
Lname = c
Salary = d
Dept_Id = e
Head_Id = f

{ a, d | (∍ b) (∍ c) (∍ e) (∍ f) (PROFESSOR(abcdef) AND b= 'Ajay' AND c ='Bhatia') }

Q2. Retrieve the name and salary of all professors who work in the 'IT' department.

The Department table is as follows:

Dept_Id	Dname	Prof_Id

Where Dept_Id = q
Dname = r
Prof Id = s

{ bcd | (∍ a) (∍ e) (∍ f) (PROFESSOR(abcdef) AND DEPARTMENT(qrs) AND r = 'IT' and e = q) }

Chapter - 4

Structured Query Language (SQL)

4.1 Structured Query Language Definition

The Structure Query Language (SQL) is the basis from which you can access a Relational Database.

The Relational Database has got rows which are known as tuples and columns in which the attributes of a record or a row is placed. The rows and columns of the relational database make a table which is more commonly known as a relation.

The Data definition of an SQL is the set of commands through which we set up the database by making tables, identifying the attributes which a table is going to have, their data type or the domain from which they will pick up values. Any modification that is necessary for the table schema i.e. to add or delete a column in an existing table or to create a new table or to destroy an existing table.

The set of commands which make up for the Data Definition of SQL are;

(1) Create Table

(2) Drop Table

(3) Alter Table

To understand the commands of SQL, we will use the following tables (given with their schemas). The schema of a table tells what the table name is going to be and what attributes it will have.

COURSE

CourseName	CourseID

STUDENT

StudentID	StudentName	Address

STUDENT_PHONES

Student_ID	Phone_no

DEPARTMENT

Dname	DeptID	Prof_Id

PROFESSOR

id	Fname	Lname	Dept_ID	Salary	Head_ID

TEACHING

Prof_ID	Course_ID	Section

STUDYING

Course_ID	Student_ID	Grade

Now to create the above tables in the database, we will have to use the CREATE TABLE command as follows;

(a)
```
CREATE TABLE COURSE (
    COURSENAME      VARCHAR(15),
    COURSEID        VARCHAR(6)       NOT NULL,
    PRIMARY KEY     ( COURSEID) );
```

(b)
```
CREATE TABLE STUDENT (
    STUDENTID       CHAR(10)         NOT NULL,
    STUDENTNAME     VARCHAR(20),
    ADDRESS         VARCHAR(50),
    PRIMARY KEY     ( STUDENTID) );
```

(c)
```
CREATE TABLE DEPARTMENT (
    DEPTID          INT              NOT NULL,
    DNAME           VARCHAR(15),
    PROF_ID         CHAR(6),
    PRIMARY KEY     (DEPTID),
    FOREIGN KEY     (PROF_ID)        REFERENCES
                    PROFESSOR        (ID));
```

(d) CREATE TABLE PROFESSOR (

```
ID              CHAR(6)         NOT NULL,
FNAME           VARCHAR(20),
LNAME           VARCHAR(20),
DEPT_ID         INT,
SALARY          DECMAL(8,2),
HEAD_ID         CHAR(6),
PRIMARY KEY     (ID),
FOREIGN KEY     (DEPT_ID)       REFERENCES
                DEPARTMENT      (DEPTID),
FOREIGN KEY     (HEAD_ID)       REFERENCES
                PROFESSOR       (ID));
```

(e) CREATE TABLE TEACHING(

```
PROF_ID         CHAR(6)         NOT NULL,
COURSE_ID       VARCHAR(6)      NOT NULL,
SECTION         CHAR(4),
PRIMARY KEY     (PROF_ID,       COURSE_ID) ,
FOREIGN KEY     (PROF_ID)       REFERENCES
                PROFESSOR       (ID),
FOREIGN KEY     COURSE_ID       REFERENCES
                COURSE          (COURSEID) );
```

(f) CREATE TABLE STUDYING (

```
COURSE_ID       VARCHAR(6)      NOT NULL,
STUDENT_ID      CHAR(10)        NOT NULL,
GRADE           DECIMAL(2,1),
PRIMARY KEY     (COURSE_ID,     STUDENT_ID)
FOREIGN KEY     (STUDENT_ID)    REFERENCES
                STUDENT         (STUDENTID)
FOREIGN KEY        COURSE_ID REFERENCES
                   COURSE (COURSEID) );
```

(g) CREATE TABLE STUDENT_PHONES(

```
STUDENT_ID      CHAR(10)          NOT NULL,
PHONE_NO        CHAR(15)          NOT NULL,
PRIMARY KEY     ( STUDENT_ID, PHONE_NO) ;
```

Here DECIMAL(2,1) means total number of decimal digits are 2 and 1 digit is after the decimal point.

The above command will create the tables in the database and space will be allocated for these tables on the SQL server.

To delete a table from the database, we will use the DROP TABLE command as follows;

(a) DROP TABLE PROFESSOR;

This will delete the PROFESSOR table from the database, the space occupied by the table will be freed and if any entries exist in the table they will also be deleted.

Similarly we can delete other tables, such as

(b) DROP TABLE TEACHING

To add or delete columns in the table, which means to change the schema of the table, we will use the ALTER TABLE command as follows;

(a) ALTER TABLE STUDENT ADD BIRTHDATE DATE;

This will change the STUDENT table's schema to;

STUDENT

StudentID	StudentName	Address	Birthdate

It will make a new column in the table with the name of BIRTHDATE and its data type or domain will be of DATE type.

To delete a column from the schema of a table we will again use the ALTER TABLE command. Suppose we want to delete the GRADE column from the STUDYING table then we will do it as follows;

(b) ALTER TABLE STUDYING DROP COLUMN GRADE;

This will make the schema of the STUDYING table as;

STUDYING

Course_ID	Student_ID

4.2 Basic Structure of SQL Queries

The basic structure of an SQL query is the

SELECT < column names >

FROM < table names >

WHERE < condition >

Clause.

In the SELECT statement, we specify the names of the attributes or the column names of the tables which we want to see in the result of the query.

In the FROM statement, we specify the tables or the relations that will be needed to select our attributes.

The WHERE clause tells us if there is any condition based on which we should select the attributes from the rows of the tables.

Some examples of the SELECT FROM WHERE clause are as follows;

(Q1) Retrieve the address of the student whose name is 'MARY KOM'.

Ans:

```
SELECT    ADDRESS
FROM      STUDENT
WHERE     STUDENTNAME = 'MARY KOM';
```

(Q2) Retrieve the name of all professors who work in 'IT' department.

Ans:

```
SELECT    FNAME, LNAME
FROM      DEPARTMENT, PROFESSOR
WHERE     DNAME = 'IT'
AND       DEPTID = DEPT_ID;
```

Here the DEPARTMENT and the PROFESSOR tables are joined by the primary key of the DEPARTMENT table DEPTID with the foreign key of the PROFESSOR table DEPT_ID.

(Q3) Select all the attributes of the professor table, who work in department number 6.

Ans:
```
SELECT    *
FROM      PROFESSOR
WHERE     DEPT_ID = 6;
```

Here* is used for selecting all attributes.

(Q4) Retrieve all students whose address is in Delhi.

Ans:
```
SELECT    STUDENTNAME
FROM      STUDENT
WHERE     ADDRESS    LIKE    '%Delhi%';
```

Here any address which has Delhi in it will be selected. The % sign before the string 'Delhi' indicates 0 or more characters can appear before 'Delhi' and the % sign after the string 'Delhi' indicates that 0 or more characters can appear after the string 'Delhi'.

(Q5) Select all students whose grade is between 4.0 nd 5.0.

Ans:
```
SELECT    STUDENTNAME, GRADE
FROM      STUDYING, STUDENT
WHERE     (GRADE BETWEEN 4.0 AND 5.0)
AND       STUDENTID = STUDENT_ID;
```

Here the BETWEEN operator along with AND operator is used to select values between 4.0 and 5.0.

4.3 Complex and Nested Queries

(Q6) Select all students who study the same courses as student whose student id is '1009013001'.

Ans:
```
SELECT    DISTINCT                       STUDENT_ID
FROM      STUDYING
WHERE     COURSE_ID IN (SELECT           COURSE_ID
                        FROM             STUDYING
                        WHERE            STUDENT_ID =
                                         '1009013001' );
```

Here the subquery selects the courses that the student with the given id studies. After that the main query matches the course ids of students with the course ids retrieved from the subquery.

(Q7) Retrieve the students who study all the courses that the student with id '1009013001' studies.

Ans:

```
SELECT  STUDENTNAME
FROM    STUDENT
WHERE   ( (SELECT   COURSE_ID
           FROM     STUDYING
           WHERE    STUDENT_
                    ID = STUDENTID)
        CONTAINS
          ( SELECT  COURSE_ID
           FROM     STUDYING
           WHERE    STUDENT_
                    ID ='1009013001') );
```

Here the subquery after contains selects all the course ids that the given student id studies. Then the subquery above contains selects all courses that are present in the result of its lower subquery. It joins the main query's STUDENT table with its STUDYING table with the condition STUDENT_ID = STUDENTID so that only those student's names are selected which satisfy the results of the subqueries.

The EXISTS clause can also be used instead of the IN operator as follows;

The difference is that we have to select the whole record with the * operator instead of a particular attribute and also with IN we are implicitly joining the attributes which we have to now do inside the subquery.

For example taking Q1 again.

(Q1) Select all students who study the same courses as student whose student id is ‘1009013001’

Ans:

```
SELECT  DISTINCT   STUDENT_ID
FROM    STUDYING   AS S1
WHERE   EXISTS     ( SELECT *
                   FROM STUDYING AS S2
                   WHERE S1.COURSE_
                   ID = S2.COURSE_ID
                   AND S2.STUDENT_
                   ID = ‘1009013001’) ;
```

Here we take two aliases of the STUDYING table as S1 and S2, since the tables have the same attribute names and we need to specify the attributes that we are joining and from which table, so we say S1.COURSE_ID which means the COURSE_ID attribute of the S1 table, which is the outer query’s STUDYING table.

Here the implicit joining of attributes which was done by the IN operator is done by the condition S1.COURSE_ID = S2.COURSE_ID.

(Q8) Select all students who study course id ‘CS-401’ and do not study course ‘CS-402’

Ans:

```
SELECT  STUDENTNAME
FROM    STUDENT
WHERE   STUDENT_ID IN (SELECT STUDENT_ID
                       FROM STUDYING
                       WHERE COURSE_
                       ID = ‘CS-401’ )
AND STUDENT_ID NOT IN (SELECT    STUDENT_ID
              FROM   STUDYING
                     WHERE COURSE_ID = ‘CS-402’ );
```

Here the students who study CS-401 and also the same students who do not study CS-402 will be selected. See the use of IN and NOT IN operators.

The STUDENT_ID field of the STUDENT table is taken and matched with the STUDENT_ID field of the STUDYING table.

(Q9) Select all students who are taught by PROF.'AJAY MARWAH'

Ans:

```
SELECT   STUDENTNAME, STUDENTID
FROM     STUDENT, TEACHING AS T, PROFESSOR,
         STUDYING AS S
WHERE    FNAME = 'AJAY'
AND      LNAME = 'MARWAH'
AND      ID = PROF_ID
AND      T. COURSE_ID = S.COURSE_ID
AND      STUDENT_ID = STUDENTID;
```

In the above, the ID field of the PROFESSOR table is matched with the PROF_ID Teaching table. Now since the COURSE_ID field name is present in both the TEACHING table as well as STUDYING table, so we have used TEACHING AS T and STUDYING AS S in the FROM statement to give an alias to both the tables. Then we specify that we are joining the COURSE_ID field of the TEACHING table as T. COURSE_ID with the COURSE_ID field of the STUDYING table as S.COURSE_ID.

Since the fields STUDENTID and STUDENT_ID differ by an underscore sign in the STUDENT AND STUDYING table so we need not give as alias and join the two tables with STUDENT_ID = STUDENTID.

4.4 Set Operations

There are 3 basic set operations in SQL;

(1) UNION

(2) INTERSECT

(3) EXCEPT or MINUS

(1) The UNION clause merges the result of two subqueries into a single table. Both the tables used in the subqueries must be union compatible that is they should have the same number of attributes and the domains of those attributes should also be the same. The UNION clause deleted duplicate rows.

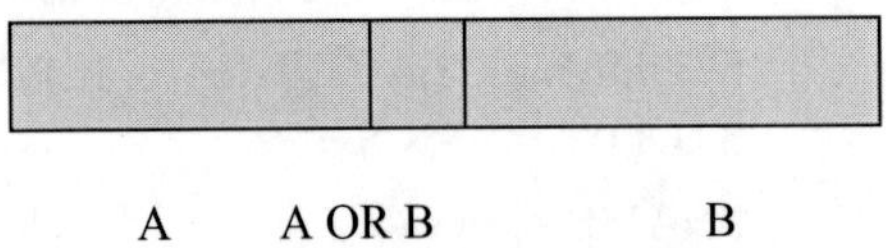

An example of the UNION clause is given below;

(Q10) Select all students who study coursed CS-401 or study coursed CS-402 or both.

Ans:

```
SELECT   STUDENTNAME
FROM     STUDENT, STUDYING
WHERE    STUDENTID = STUDENT_ID
AND      COURSE_ID = 'CS-401'
UNION
SELECT   STUDENTNAME
FROM     STUDENT, STUDYING
WHERE    STUDENTID = STUDENT_ID
AND      COURSE_ID = 'CS-402' ;
```

(2) The INTERSECT clause picks the result from both the subqueries and those results which appear in both the subqueries or are common to both subqueries are finally selected.

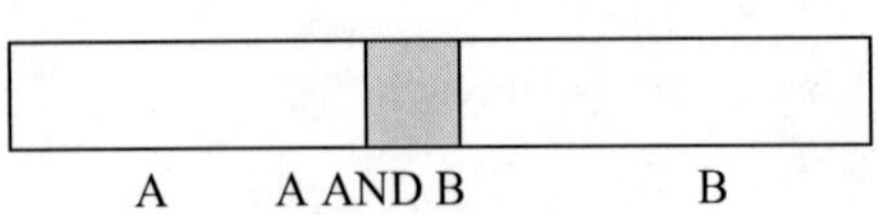

An example of the INTERSECT clause is given below;

(Q11) Select all students who study both the courses 'CS-401' and 'CS-402'.

Ans:

```
SELECT   STUDNTNAME
FROM     STUDENT, STUDYING
WHERE    STUDENTID = STUDENT_ID
AND      COURSE_ID = 'CS-401'

INTERSECT
SELECT   STUDENTNAME
FROM     STUDENT, STUDYING
WHERE    STUDENTID = STUDENT_ID
AND      COURSE_ID = 'CS-402';
```

Here it will select only those students who study both these courses at the same time.

(3) The EXCEPT or MINUS clause selects the rows of one subquery and makes sure that the final result does not appear in the result of the second subquery.

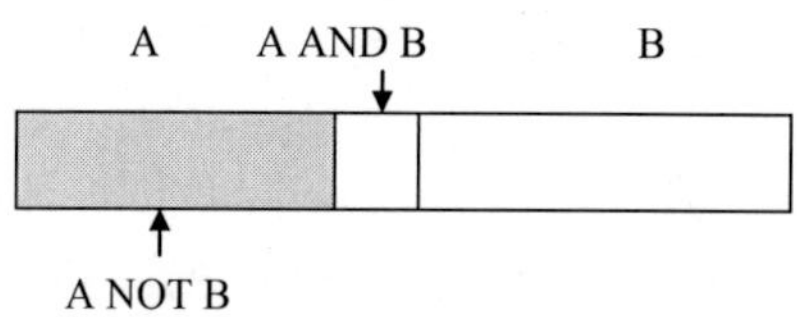

An example of the EXCEPT clause is given below;

(Q12) Select the names of the students who do not study course id 'CS-401'.

Ans:

```
SELECT   STUDENTNAME, STUDENTID
FROM     STUDENT

EXCEPT
SELECT   STUDENTNAME, STUDENTID
FROM     STUDENT, STUDYING
```

```
WHERE    STUDENTID = STUDENT_ID
AND      COURSE_ID = 'CS-401';
```

Here the subquery selects all students who study course id 'CS-401'. The main query selects all the students who study any course. Then the EXCEPT clause deletes those students who study course id 'CS-401' from all the students and this gives us those students who do not study course id 'CS-401';

4.5 Aggregate Functions

Aggregate functions are used to get a collection of values from the database by grouping them on some attribute. For example we may need to count some number of tuples which satisfy a particular condition. We may need to find the sum or average of some numeric attributes or we may need to find a maximum or minimum value that exists in the database for a particular numeric attribute. For that SQL provides the following set of aggregate functions;

(1) COUNT

(2) SUM

(3) AVG

(4) MIN

(5) MAX

To understand them we will take the help of some examples.

(Q13) Retrieve the total number of students in the institute.

Ans:

```
SELECT   COUNT(*)
FROM     STUDENT;
```

We know that the STUDENT table has a unique entry for each student. So we apply the COUNT function and get the total number of students. Remember the COUNT function is always applied on the whole record specified by the * operator.

(Q14) Find the sum of the salaries of all professors, also their minimum salary, their maximum salary and their average alary.

Ans:

```
SELECT   SUM(SALARY), MAX(SALARY),
         MIN(SALARY), AVG(SALARY)
```

```
FROM      PROFESSOR;
```

Remember the SUM, AVG, MIN and MAX functions are always applied on numeric attributes. So salary is a numeric attribute, therefore we can use the above mentioned functions with it.

(Q15) Count the number of students who study the course 'CS-401';

Ans:

```
SELECT    COUNT(*)
FROM      STUDYING
WHERE     COURSE_ID = 'CS-401';
```

Here we know that the STUDYING table will have a unique entry for each student with each course, so we select the rows in which course id 'CS-401' appears and that gives us the number of students studying that course.

(Q16) Find the number of professors who work in the 'IT' department.

Ans:

```
SELECT    COUNT(*)
FROM      DEPARTMENT, PROFESSOR
WHERE     DEPTID= DEPT_ID
AND       DNAME = 'IT';
```

(Q17) Find the sum of the salaries of all professors who work in 'IT' department as well as the minimum, the maximum and the average salary of all professors of 'IT' department.

Ans:

```
SELECT    SUM(SALARY), AVG(SALARY),
          MIN(SALARY)  MAX(SALARY)
FROM      PROFESSOR, DEPARTMENT
WHERE     DEPTID = DEPT_ID
AND       DNAME = 'IT';
```

4.5.1 USING GROUP BY CLAUSE IN AGGREGATE FUNCTIONS

Sometimes we may need to find the sum, the average or the count of the number of tuples based on a particular attribute.

For example:

(Q18) Retrieve the number of courses that each student studies.

Ans:

```
SELECT      STUDENT_ID, COUNT(*)
FROM        STUDYING
GROUP BY    STUDENT_ID;
```

We know in the STUDYING table there is one row for each student and the course he studies. So if we group by the STUDENT_ID. That is by the student himself, we will get the total number of rows or courses that he studies.

Then we display the student's id and the number of rows in his student id group. So we get a list of all students and the number of courses they study.

(Q19) Find the average salary and the sum of all the salaries of professors working in each department.

Ans:

```
SELECT      DEPT_ID, AVG(SALARY),
            SUM(SALARY)
FROM        PROFESSOR
GROUP BY    DEPT_ID;
```

Here it will display each department's id and the average salary and the sum of the salaries of each department.

Suppose now we want to know how many professors work in each department and also we display the name of each department with it.

(Q20) For each department display the department's id, the department name and the number of professors who belong to that department.

Ans:

```
SELECT      DEPT_ID, DNAME, COUNT(*)
FROM        DEPARTMENT, PROFESSOR
WHERE       DEPTID = DEPT_ID
GROUP BY    DEPT_ID, DNAME;
```

4.5.2 USING HAVING WITH GROUP BY CLAUSE IN AGGREGATE FUNCTIONS

HAVING clause is used with GROUP BY clause and not on its own. The use of HAVING clause is that if we want to attach some condition with the GROUP BY clause, we will have to use the HAVING clause.

Suppose we want to know how many professors teach more than 3 courses. For that we will have to write a query like this.

(Q21) For each professor who teaches more than 3 courses, display his name and his id.

Ans:
```
SELECT      ID, FNAME, LNAME, COUNT(*)
FROM        PROFESSOR, TEACHING
WHERE       ID = PROF_ID
GROUP BY    ID, FNAME, LNAME
HAVING      COUNT(*) >= 3;
```

Here the PROFESSOR and the TEACHING table will be joined on the ids of the professors, and then they will be grouped by the professors's id, fname and lname. So each professor and his courses will be in one group, then we will count the number of rows which appear for each professor and all those whose rows are 3 or more than 3 will be displayed. Since we have counted the number of rows by COUNT(*) in the SELECT clause and put the condition in the HAVING clause that the COUNT(*) should be equal to or more than 3.

4.6 NULL Values

NULL values are those in which we cannot put any competent value from its domain but it need to be NULL.

Sometimes NULL values cannot be avoided. For example,

Suppose that our STUDENT table had the schema

Studentid	Studentname	Address	PhoneNo

Suppose the student does not have a phone number, which is very unlikely in today's world, but let us assume that some students have phone numbers and some students do not have phone numbers. So the students who do not have phone numbers, we will have to put a NULL value in phone no field of their respective records.

Normally our database does not allow our primary keys to contain NULL values. Since we have to search our tables on the primary key attribute and if that attribute is NULL, we will not be able to retrieve any record.

Also you must have noticed that when we created our tables with CREATE table command, we put a constraint of NOT NULL with the primary key. Which means that while inserting records in the database, if by mistake we enter a NULL value in the primary key attribute then the system will not accept that record and raise an error.

But sometimes we have to put a NULL value in our fields and there is no other choice but to put a null value.

For example, consider the PROFESSOR schema

Id	Fname	Lname	Dept_ID	Salary	Head_Id

Now in this case the ID field is the primary key of our professor whose record this is. The HEAD_ID is the id of the professor who is the head of this professor. So for professors who work under someone will have will have a value in their HEAD_ID field. But a professor who is already working as a head and does not have anyone on top of him will have a NULL value in his HEAD_ID field, but his ID field will be his primary key and he will be identified with his ID field.

Now suppose we want to know the names of all heads of departments. Then their HEAD_ID field will be NULL, so we can search on that.

(Q22) List the IDs and the Names of all the heads of departments.

Ans:
```
SELECT    ID, FNAME, LNAME
FROM      PROFESSOR
WHERE     HEAD_ID is NULL;
```

4.7 Modification of the Database

The modification of the database is done via Data manipulation Language commands such as INSERT, DELETE and UPDATE. This is how we change the values inside the tables or insert or delete records inside the tables. This is known as changing the extension of the database whereas in the Data Definition Language, we had the commands CREATE TABLE, DROP TABLE and ALTER TABLE, where we changed the schemas of the database or the intension of the database. In Data Definition Language we created the tables, now in Data Manipulation Language we are going to populate the tables.

Modification of the database is done by

(1) The INSERT command

(2) The DELETE command

(3) The UPDATE command

(1) The INSERT command is used to insert a record into the table with specifying the values of each attribute in the same order in which the table was created and the values should be from the domains or the data types that was specified at the time of creating the attributes within the table.

For Example,

Let us insert a record into the PROFESSOR table, the PROFESSOR table had the fields in the order of ID, FNAME, LNAME, DEPT_ID, SALARY and HEAD_ID with the data types of these attributes as CHAR(6), VARCHAR(20), VARCHAR(20), INT, DECIMAL(8,2) and CHAR(6) respectively.

This can be done as follows:

INSERT INTO PROFESSOR VALUES

('101102', 'Ajay', 'Marwah', 2, 32000, '160021');

Since the ID field is CHAR and FNAME and LNAME fields are VARCHAR, therefore they are given in single quotes. The DEPT_ID is INT and SALARY is DECIMAL therefore they are single numeric and do not need any quotes. The HEAD_ID is CHAR and therefore it needs single quotes.

We can give similar INSERT statements to insert a record for every professor and similarly we can give INSERT statements to populate other tables such as STUDENT, STUDYING etc.

(2) The DELETE command is used to delete a record or a row or a tuple from an existing table which was already populated by some INSERT statement before.

For Example,

(Q23) Delete a student whose name is 'Jaikishan'.

Ans:
```
DELETE    FROM    STUDENT
WHERE     STUDENTNAME = 'Jaikishan';
```

This will remove the entry of the STUDENT with the name 'Jaikishan' from the STUDENT table. If there are 2 students with the same name as 'Jaikishan', then both of them will be removed. Therefore if we want to delete only one unique record then we should always give the condition equating the primary key of that table in the WHERE statement of the DELETE clause.

If we want to delete all entries from the table but we want the table to remain in the database we will have to specify like this.

```
DELETE    FROM    STUDENT
```

This will delete all entries of the STUDENT table and remember if we want to delete the table from the database, we will have to specify the DROP TABLE command.

(3) The UPDATE command is used to change the value of an attribute with the existing records of a table in the database.

For Example if we want to modify the SALARY of a professor who has just got an increment and wants to update his SALARY field only, the rest of the details of the professor are just as it is. For that we have to give something like this:

(Q24) Update the salary of the professor to 40000 whose id is '101102'.

Ans:

```
UPDATE    PROFESSOR
SET       SALARY = 40000
WHERE     ID = '101102';
```

Here only the professor whose id is '101102' will have his salary attribute updated. The rest of the fields will remain the same.

Here we are specifying the id instead of the name of the professor because it is the primary key of the PROFESSOR table and is unique. Otherwise if we had 2 professors with the same name and then if we give the name of the professor in the WHERE statement, then both the professors' salaries will be changed.

4.8 Join Expressions

There are 2 types of Join Expressions:

(1) The INNER Join

(2) The OUTER Join

Till now the joins that we have specified in the queries above has been a type of inner join expression.

In an inner join expression, we select the rows from both the tables where the join condition matches on both attributes of the tables.

For Example, refer to query no 2.

(Q2) Retrieve the name of all professors who work in 'IT' department.

Ans:

```
SELECT    FNAME, LNAME
FROM      DEPARTMENT, PROFESSOR
WHERE     DNAME = 'IT'
AND       DEPTID = DEPT_ID;
```

Now here the inner join expression is specified by the statement DEPTID = DEPT_ID. The DEPTID exists in the DEPARTMENT table and is the primary key of that table, whereas the DEPT_ID exists in the PROFESSOR table and is the foreign key of the PROFESSOR table referencing the primary key DEPTID of the department table.

The row of the DEPARTMENT table in which the value of the DEPTID field matches with the DEPT_ID field of the PROFESSOR table's row are joined to make a single row and that's how the rows will be selected from the two tables. On those selected rows only those rows whose DNAME is 'IT' will be further selected and then from there the name of the professors will be given as the result.

So in an inner join, both the fields DEPTID and DEPT_ID from two tables are matched on common values and only when the match is there, the rows are taken as part of the selected rows.

In an OUTER join, the rows are selected from the two tables, even if the match is there or not.

There are 3 types of OUTER joins:

(1) LEFT OUTER JOIN

(2) RIGHT OUTER JOIN

(3) FULL OUTER JOIN

(1) In a LEFT OUTER join the table on the left hand side will select all rows irrespective of the fact whether a match of the 2 fields is there or not.

For Example, we say

We want to select al the professor names and their department names.

```
SELECT      FNAME, LNAME, DNAME
FROM        PROFESSOR LEFT OUTER JOIN
            DEPARTMENT ON DEPT_ID = DEPTID;
```

Now here the left table is PROFESSOR and the right table is DEPARTMENT and the join is LEFT OUTER JOIN.

So this means that all values of the professor's names will be selected from the PROFESSOR table, even if the professor does not belong to any department. If he belongs to to a department then his name and the department's name will be listed otherwise if he does not belong to a department, it will show only his name and a NULL value for the department's name.

(2) Similarly we can specify a RIGHT OUTER JOIN, in which the table on the right hand side will display all the values irrespective of the fact whether a match of the field is there or not. In case a match is there, it will display values from both the tables otherwise it will display a NULL value of the left hand side table and a normal value of the right hand side table.

Suppose we give the query as:

```
SELECT    FNAME, LNAME, DNAME
FROM      PROFSSOR RIGHT OUTER JOIN DEPARTMENT
          ON DEPT_ID = DEPTID;
```

Then if there are some departments which do not have any professors in them then the names of all the departments will be listed and the name of the professors will be NULL in those cases where there are no professors in the departments. In the cases where the departments have professors they will list both the FNAME, LNAME and DNAME i.e. the name of the professor and the name of the department.

(3) FULL OUTER JOIN combines the effect of a right outer join with a left outer join. In this case we can have NULL values for both the tables.

4.9 Views

Views are commonly known as virtual tables. They are used for ready reference. When we give a CREATE TABLE command, then physically the space is created for the table and we can insert records in that space. In case of a view we may join two tables and pick up some attributes which need to be referenced again and again and create a view of that. In this case no physical space will be allocated to the view, it will take the values from the underlying tables and just create a kind of a virtual table or we may refer to it as a report.

There are two cases here, one is that the view does not have a space of its own and the other is that it is saved temporarily in a physically created view for future reference.

But in either of the two cases, the underlying advantage of creating a view is that we save time in joining the tables whenever we want to refer to them. If the things we need to look at again and again, then we may create views of those and use the views instead of tables to select further information from them.

Suppose we want to know the names of the students who study certain courses. Then we may create the view of the STUDENT table and the STUDYING table and the COURSE table, so that we can prevent the joins of these tables again and again.

We may do this as follows by creating a view:

```
CREATE   VIEW STUDIES AS
SELECT   STUDENTNAME, COURSENAME, GRADE
FROM     COURSE, STUDENT, STUDYING
WHERE    STUDENTID = STUDENT_ID
AND      COURSEID = COURSE_ID;
```

Now if we want to know the names of all students who study COURSENAME = 'DATA STRUCTURES' then we can write like this:

```
SELECT   STUDENTNAME
FROM     STUDIES
WHERE    COURSENAME = 'DATA STRUCTURES';
```

Remember STUDIES is the name of the view we just created.

4.10 Accessing SQL from a Programming Language

Till now we have seen that SQL can be accessed by giving DDL and DML statements on the SQL prompt and access the SQL database from there.

But there are techniques in which we can embed the SQL into a program and run that program and from inside the program we will be able to access the SQL database and get answer for our queries.

Another method is to write a file which is full of SQL commands and then run the file with the help of @<filename>. The list of commands given inside the file will be executed and their results displayed on screen.

The @<filename> can be run using an interactive interface. The interactive interface where you run usual SQL commands can be used for ad-hoc queries but where data has to be dealt in large volumes or complexities are involved then database programming needs to be done.

There are 2 approaches in which database programming can be carried out.

(1) The database commands are embedded into a programming language.

Here the programming language is called the host language program and the SQL commands are written in this host language program. To identify that this particular statement is an SQL command and is different from the other statements of the program. A keyword EXEC SQL is written before beginning the SQL command. The preprocessor first scans the host language program to identify all statements that have SQL commands. These statements are given to the DBMS for processing. Their answers are returned to the program.

(2) A library of database functions is used.

Here through the Application Programming Interface (API), the functions to the database are called, the functions can have input parameters as required. These functions call the database for making connections to the database or to execute a query or to make an update to the database or to delete a table and so on.

Because the database model differs from the programming language model, there occurs a problem known as Impedance Mismatch. In

Impedance Mismatch, take an example of say a relational model. In relational model we have 3 types of constructs:

(1) The attributes and their datatypes.

(2) The tuples or records.

(3) The tables or multiple set of records.

Now these attributes differ from the data types of the programming language.

Now we need to bind the attributes of the relational model data types i.e. SQL data types i.e. SQL data types to the host programming language data types. For example the data types of C and JAVA are different and again both of them are different from the relational model data type i.e. SQL data type.

The 2nd problem occurs when the results of the query gives a number of records and each record is made of a number of attributes with different data types. So we need a method to capture the result of the query and put values of attributes into respective variables defined for them. So we need to loop over the number of records returned by the query and here we require a cursor which is also known as the iterator variable which is used for looping over the result of query to get each individual record of the query.

PL/SQL is an example of a special database programming language that is designed to have data types same as those of the data types of the database model.

In database programming, the common Client Server Paradigm is used.

(1) The client establishes a connection with the server.

(2) Once the connection is established, client makes requests to the server. The server responds with the results of the queries being made.

(3) Once the interaction is over, the client closes the connection with the server.

4.10.1 Embedded SQL

The SQL statements when written in any programming language are said to be embedded in that language such as C, COBOL, ADA etc. This language is known as the host language and to distinguish the SQL statements from other statements of the program, the SQL statements are prefixed by a keyword known as EXEC SQL. When the preprocessor compiles the program, it comes to know that this is an SQL statement and has to be dealt with the database. We can write DML statements and VIEW and CONSTRAINT definition statements within the SQL statements.

The END EXEC keyword is used to mark the end of the SQL statements block or they can simply be ended by giving a semi colon (;).

We take the example of C language as the host language.

In this we use shared variables which can be used both as normal program variables and variables of the SQL statements to capture the attribute names and relation names.

The way that these variables are distinguished from a normal program variable and SQL variable is that as a program variable they are written normally and as an SQL variable they are written with a colon (:) preceding them.

For Example, let us use the example of our STUDENT and PROFESSOR tables referred to in earlier sections.

We may write our code as follows:

```
int count;
EXEC SQL BEGIN DECLARE SECTION;
     varchar studid[10], studname[20], address[50], pname[20],
     dname[15], name[20] ;
     char profid[6], id[6];
     int deptid, dno;
     float          salary, bonus;
     int            SQLCODE;
     char           SQLSTATE[6];
EXEC SQL END DECLARE SECTION;
```

We may use the *studid* variable in both ways as a program variable and as an SQL variable as follows:

```
prompt("enter the student id : ", studid);
EXEC SQL
    SELECT          STUDENTNAME
    INTO       : studname
    FROM       STUDENT
    WHERE           STUDENTID = :studid ;
    IF              ( SQLCODE = = 0)
    printf(studname)
    ELSE
    printf("Student Id is not there", studid);
```

Now the DECLARE section is used to declare all shared variables with their different data types.

The SQLCODE and SQLSTATE are known as communication variables because they communicate between the SQL Database and the application program.

After each SQL command a value is returned in the SQLCODE variable and a 0 value indicates that the SQL command was successful. If the value of SQLCODE is less than 0, it indicates that there was an error while executing the given SQL command.

Now in the above case, we entered the student's id by the prompt statement and put it in the variable *studid,* we got the student name of that student id from the STUDENT table by giving the SQL SELECT FROM WHERE statement. When it is used in the SQL statement *studid* variable is preceded with a colon (:) and as a program variable in printf or prompt statement it is used without a colon.

The variables that are required to be used only in the program and not in any SQL statement are declared before the SQL DECLARE section and not inside it.

The SQLSTATE variable indicates an error or an exception condition. That is if an error has occurred then what was the nature of the exception. SQLSTATE is a string containing 5 characters. A value of "00000" in SQLSTATE indicates no error or exception, other values indicate various errors or exceptions. Another example of a string say "02000" tells that no more data is present.

The INTO clause tells in which program variable the attributes retrieved from the database should be stored.

4.10.2 USING CURSORS

Cursors are used where multiple rows are retrieved from the database. Cursors are used to point to the current row of the rows retrieved from the database which are the result of a given query.

The cursor points to the current row, you can make updates to that row and then the cursor will move to the next row of the result of the query and then you can make changes to that row and so on. The cursor reaches the last row of the result of the query.

This can be done with the help of 4 statements:

(1) The DECLARE CURSOR statement

(2) The OPEN CURSOR statement

(3) The FETCH FROM cursor INTO statement

(4) The CLOSE CURSOR statement

Let us take the following example from our previous database to understand the function of the cursors.

Suppose we want to give certain bonus to the professors of a given department which have shown good results.

This can be done with the following code:

```
prompt("Enter the name of the Department which has to be given increments:", dname);

EXEC SQL
    SELECT    DEPTID INTO :dno
    FROM      DEPARTMENT
    WHERE     DNAME = :dname ;
```

```
EXEC SQL DECLARE PROF CURSOR FOR
    SELECT      ID, FNAME, LNAME, SALARY
    FROM        PROFESSOR
    WHERE       DEPT_ID = :dno
    FOR UPDATE OF SALARY;
EXEC SQL OPEN PROF;
EXEC SQL FETCH FROM PROF INTO : id, :fname, :lname,
:salary; while (SQLCODE = = 0)
{
printf("Professor Name is :", fname, lname);
prompt ("Enter the bonus amount :", bonus);
EXEC SQL
    UPDATE      PROFESSOR
    SET         SALARY = SALARY + bonus
    WHERE       CURRENT OF PROF ;
EXEC SQL FETCH FROM PROF INTO : id, :fname, :lname,
:salary;}
EXEC SQL CLOSE PROF;
```

In the above case, first we ask the user to enter the name of the department in which you want to give increments. Then with EXEC SQL statement we get the DEPT_ID captured in the *dno* variable. For the department name which was given earlier in the *dname* variable.

Then with EXEC SQL DECLARE PROF FOR statement we are creating the cursor named PROF for getting the id, fname, lname and salary of all the professors belonging to that department. We also say FOR UPADTE OF SALARY to indicate the purpose of cursor.

The SELECT FROM WHERE statement in the DECLARE CURSOR FOR statement is executed and we get the result of the query.

We now open our cursor PROF with the EXEC SQL OPEN PROF statement to indicate that we are starting our work with cursors.

The current row is fetched from the multiple rows returned as the result of the query with the help of the EXEC SQL FETCH FROM PROF INTO statement. The attributes of the row are put into the desired variables.

If the fetch was successful then our communication variable SQLCODE will return a value of 0. After checking the SQLCODE we ask the name of the professor to whom bonus is to be given, then we ask for the bonus amount.

Then with EXEC SQL UPDATE statement we update the salary of the professor by adding bonus to the current salary and here we write WHERE CURRENT OF PROF to indicate that the changes are to be made where the current row of the cursor PROF is.

After the update is done, we again give the EXEC SQL FETCH statement so that the cursor goes to the next row of the result of the query and fetches new values into the variables and that row now becomes the current row of the cursor.

Like this it is repeated in the while loop till all rows have been updated and that will be indicated by the SQLCODE = = 0 statement.

The cursor variable PROF in this case acts as an iterator which goes from one row to the next until all rows are covered. Then the CLOSE CURSOR statement tells that we have finished our work with the cursor variable.

4.11 Functions and Procedures

In database programming, we can use functions and procedures to enhance the capability of our programs. These functions and procedures are stored at the server end. In a client server paradigm where the client machinesaccepts the requests, processes it and replies the answer or the result of the query back to the client machine.

These procedures are stored permanently on the server machine which were earlier known as database stored procedures. The SQL term used to describe such procedures id SQL/PSM or SQL Persistent Stored Modules. Persistent means which continue to exist for a long period of time.

The procedures stored at the server end can be invoked any time by any client. They help to reduce the network traffic if they are executed at server end. The most important aspect of the procedures and functions is that any kind of capability or checking of constraints or any other complex situation can be programmed into them which can otherwise not be handled.

The syntax of a procedure is as follows:

CREATE PROCEDURE < name of procedure> (<list of parameters>)

<local variable declarations >

<procedure code> ;

This CREATE PROCEDURE can be written directly from the SQL prompt or can be written in a general purpose programming language. Similarly we can create the functions as follows with the only difference that they have a return type, just as in the case of any programming language.

The syntax of the function is as follows:

CREATE FUNCTION< name of function > (< list of parameters >) RETURNS < return type >

<local variable declarations >

<function code > ;

If the procedure or function is written in a general purpose programming language then it is necessary to tell the name of the language and the name of the file in which the function or procedure is stored.

This may be written as

CREATE PROCEDURE < name of procedure > (< list of parameters >)

LANGUAGE < name of programming language >

EXTERNAL NAME < name of the file with path >

The list of parameters generally indicates the parameter types which correspond to the SQL data types, also with each parameter type it is necessary to specify the IN OUT and INOUT keywords indicating whether it is to be used as an input, output or both input output variable respectively.

Now once your procedures or functions have been created and are stored on the server. There should be a method to invoke them or call them. This is done with the help of the CALL statement, which can be directly written onto the SQL prompt or written inside a host programming language using embedded SQL.

The syntax of a CALL statement is as follows:

CALL < procedure or function name >(< list of parameters >)

The function or procedures can have the normal programming language constructs such as IF –ELSE, REPEAT UNTIL, WHILE DO and FOR LOOP.

The syntax of the constructs is given below:

(1) IF < condition > THEN < set of statements>
    ELSEIF < condition > THEN < set of statements>
    ELSEIF < condition > THEN < set of statements>
    ELSE < set of statements>
    END IF ;

(2) REPEAT
    <set of statements >
    UNTIL < condition >
    END REPEAT ;

(3) WHILE < condition > DO
    <set of statements >
    END WHILE ;

4) FOR < name of loop > AS < name of cursor > CURSOR FOR
    <query> DO
    <set of statements >
    END FOR;

An example indicating the above constructs:

Suppose we want to know in how many subjects a student got the grade of 5.0. If he got a grade of 5.0 in more than 5 subjects then we return a value "OUTSTANDING". If he got a grade of 5.0 in more than 4 subjects then we return a value "EXCELLENT". If he got a grade of 5.0 in more than 3 subjects then we return a value "GOOD" otherwise we return a value "AVERAGE".

To solve the above question using functions we would write it as follows:

```
CREATE FUNCTION status (IN studid char[10])
RETURNS varchar[15]

DECLARE noofsubs integer;
SELECT   COUNT(*) INTO noofsubs
FROM     STUDYING
WHERE    STUDENT_ID = studid
AND      GRADE = 5.0;

IF noofsubs> 5 THEN RETURN "OUTSTANDING"
    ELSEIF noofsubs> 4 THEN RETURN "EXCELLENT"
    ELSEIF noofsubs> 3 THEN RETURN "GOOD"
    ELSE RETURN "AVERAGE"

END IF;
```

Now in the above case, the name of our function is *status*. We take an IN parameter *studid* to get the student id for only input purpose.

The function returns a string type. The variable *noofsubs* is used to count the number of subjects in which the student got the grade of 5.0.

This is done by the SELECT FROM WHERE statement. The value of the variable *noofsubs* is compared, if it is greater than 5 then the function returns the string "OUTSTANDING". If it was more than 4 then the function returns the string "EXCELLENT". If it was more than 3 then it returns "GOOD" otherwise it returns "AVERAGE".

Chapter - 5

Functional Dependencies and Normalization

5.1 Introduction

Normalization is the process in which we decomposethe tables into proper tables such that no data redundancy or no inconsistency exists in the Database.

Also with Normalization we are able to put the attributes in the proper tables such that no insertion, updation or deletion anomalies exist and no attribute occurs in 2 different tables, only there might be primary key foreign key references.

There are ways in which the attributes of the database may be organized into proper tables. Some are based on intuitions, others based on looking at the tables and finding the right place of the attributes.

Bu the most formal way in which we can normalize the tables are based on functional dependencies.

Functional dependencies are the mathematical, logical way of organizing the tables with proper attributes.

The process of Normalization consists of putting the tables into Normal Forms. The sequence of Normal Forms is as follows:

(1) First Normal Form (1NF)

(2) Second Normal Form (2NF)

(3) Third Normal Form (3NF)

(4) Boyce Codd Normal Form (BCNF)

(5) Fourth Normal Form (4NF)

(6) Fifth Normal Form (5NF)

Atable will be in next higher Normal Form if it is already in the lower Normal Form. For Example, a table will be in Second Normal Form if it is already in First Normal Form. A table will be in Third Normal Form if it is in Second Normal Form.

We will describe the functional dependencies later, first le us see what is the need of Normalization, why should we go through the process of putting the tablesinto various Normal Forms. What is it that exists that we hould have a proper place for every attribute in tables.

5.2 Updation Anomalies

The answer to the above question is that there exists some kind of anomalies, if we just group some attributes together and put it into tables. Then some problems may arise. And those problems are called updation anomalies which exists in 3 forms:

(1) Insertion Anomalies

(2) Deletion Anomalies

(3) Modification Anomalies.

5.2.1 Insertion Anomalies

Consider the following table:

PROFESSOR_DEPT

ID	NAME	DEPT_ID	SALARY	HEAD_ID	DNAME	DNUMBER	DLOCATION

All those attributes are present in one table called PROFESSOR_ DEPT with the primary key od ID.

(a) Suppose a new professor joins the institute and has not yet been assigned any department. Then we may enter his details as

PROFESSOR_DEPT

ID	NAME	DEPT_ID	SALARY	HEAD_ID	DNAME	DNUMBER	DLOCATION
1096	Dr. Jain	NULL	60000	4096	NULL	NULL	NULL

So there are a lot of null values specially of the fields of the department that is DNAME, DNUMBER and DLOCATION, which may not be desirable because we don't want to keep too many NULL values in our database.

(b) Now assume that a new department 'MBA' has been created and its dnumber is 'D0081'and its location is 'Delhi'. But we do not have any Professor working in it as yet. So our database will look like this.

PROFESSOR_DEPT

ID	NAME	DEPT_ID	SALARY	HEAD_ID	DNAME	DNUMBER	DLOCATION
NULL	NULL	NULL	NULL	NULL	MBA	D0081	DELHI

So again there are a lot of NULL values in the database which are not desirable.

So this is the Insertion Anomaly that if we want to enter a new record of a new Department, we must have a Professor working in it otherwise we will have to enter all NULL values for the fields or attributes describing Professor. This is not suitable for a database to have a lot of NULL values as it indicates a poor design and consumes lot of space.

5.2.2 Deletion Anomalies

Consider the following Database

PROFESSOR_DEPT

ID	NAME	DEPT_ID	SALARY	HEAD_ID	DNAME	DNUMBER	DLOCATION
101	Mr. Jain	D0011	20000	102	IT	D0011	DELHI
102	Ms. Jaya	D0011	60000	NULL	IT	D0011	BOMBAY
103	Mr. Yadav	D0022	40000	101	MBA	D0022	DELHI
104	Mr. Garg	D0024	30000	102	CIVIL	D0024	CALCUTTA
105	Ms. Mala	D0026	50000	104	CS	D0026	MADRAS

Now suppose our 'MBA' Department has been closed down and we want to delete its entry. So we will have to remove the whole record containing 'MBA' department. Which is

103	Mr. Yadav	D0022	40000	101	MBA	D0022	DELHI

So with deleting the 'MBA' dept, we are losing all the information of the Professor with ID '103' and Name 'Mr. Yadav'

So this is not reasonable , may be a department has closed down but the professor has not resigned and he is still with the institute. Maybe the institute plans to transfer him to another department. So why should we lose his information altogether.

This is simple because his information is existing with the 'MBA' department and if the 'MBA ' department's information is deleted the professor's information may be lost automatically.

So this is the Deletion Anomaly that wanting to delete some information, other information is lost automatically.

5.2.3 Modification Anomalies

Consider the following database:

ID	NAME	DEPT_ID	SALARY	HEAD_ID	DNAME	DNUMBER	DLOCATION
101	Mr. Jain	D0011	20000	102	IT	D0011	DELHI
102	Ms. Jaya	D0011	60000	NULL	IT	D0011	BOMBAY
103	Mr. Yadav	D0022	40000	101	MBA	D0022	DELHI
104	Mr. Garg	D0024	30000	102	CIVIL	D0024	CALCUTTA
105	Ms. Mala	D0026	50000	104	CS	D0026	MADRAS
106	Ms. Lata	D0026	30000	104	CS	D0026	DELHI

Now suppose the institute wishes to change he name of its Department Computer Science (CS) to Computer Science Engineering (CSE). So we will have to change it at 2 places. That is in the record of ID '105' NAME 'Ms. Mala' and record of ID '106' NAME 'Ms. Lata'

In the Column DNAME we need to put 'CSE' instead of 'CS' which is already existing.

Suppose we change in 'Ms. Mala' 's record but forget to change in 'MsLata' 's record . So our database will be in an inconsistent state. At one place it is showing 'CSE' and at another place it is showing 'CS' whereas both refer to the same department number ' D0026'

The inconsistency will be shown as follows

105	Ms. Mala	D0026	50000	104	CSE	D0026	MADRAS
106	Ms. Lata	D0026	30000	104	CS	D0026	DELHI

So this is Modification Anomaly that changes at all places have not occurred correctly and that is why the database state is inconsistent.

5.3 Functional Dependencies

A functional dependency is normally given by the following notation

X -> Y

Which is in other words quoted as X determines Y where X and Y are attributes of a relation or we can say in other words Y is dependent on X for its values.

More formally it is stated as if there are 2 tuples t1 and t2

If the value of X in t1 is equal to the value of X in t2

t1[X] = t2[X]

Then the value of Y in t1 must be equal to the value of Y in t2 , or it can be written as

t1[Y] = t2[Y]

We are trying to say that if the value of X in a tuuple (t1) or a row or record is some value, and the same value of X iss present in another tuple (t2) or row or record.

Then whatever value of Y exists in the tuple t1, the same value of Y must exist in tuple t2.

Now take for an example that we have a student relation.

In this STUDENT_MARKS relation we have the following seet of attributes.

ROLL_NO	STUDENT_NAME	SUBJECT	MARKS

Now we have a functional dependency that exists as follows :

ROLL_NO -> STUDENT_NAME

In this case our X attribute is ROLL_NO and our Y attribute is STUDENT_NAME So we have 2 tuples t1 nad t2 such that

	ROLL_NO	STUDENT_NAME	SUBJECT	MARKS
t1	1509010001	Rita Sharma	DBMS	74
t2	1509010001	Rita Sharma	OS	86

Then the constraint t1[X] = t2[X] must follow that t1[Y] = t2[Y]

So here we have t1[X] value is 1509010001 and

t2[X] value is 1509010001

and our Y also agrees t1[Y] = Rita Sharma and

t2[Y] = Rita Sharma

In other words if X is determining Y, then whenever there is some value of X that gives a value of Y, in any other row we cannot have the same value of X giving some other value of Y. It has to give the same previous value of Y.

Here the ROLL_NO -> STUDENT_NAME

So whenever a student is having a particular ROLL_NO, his name will be the same. We cannot have one ROLL_NO giving 2 different names.

Or in other words we cannot have

	ROLL_NO	STUDENT_NAME	SUBJECT	MARKS
t1	1509010001	Rita Sharma	DBMS	74
t2	1509010001	SitaVerma	OS	86

The above is not possible, so whenever the ROLL_NO exists with a particular name , in another row the same ROLL_NO cannot exist with another name.

5.3.1 Inference Rules for Functional Depenedencies

Inference Rules means those rules which can be applied to functional dependencies to find out or infer more functional dependencies.

From a set F of functional dependencies, if we want to infer all the functional dependencies then we have to find the closure of F.

The formal definition of a closure of F says that the set of depepndencies that are included in F and all the other dependencies that are inferred from F is known as the closure of F and is denoted by F^+.

To get the closure of F that is { F^+ }, we must have a proper way to determine how other dependencies can be inferred from the already given dependencie in F.

The Inference Rules are a way which give us the proper method to infer other dependencies of F.

There are in total 6 inference rules for functional dependencies:

1. The Reflexive Rule: It states that if X is a superset of Y then X functionally determines Y or in other words it is written as

   If X -> Y, then X -> Y
2. The Augmentation Rule: It states that if an attribute Z is augmented on both sides of a functional dependency, X ->Y, then that functional dependency also holds. Or in other words it is written as

   { X -> Y } FOLLOWS XZ -> YZ
3. The Transitive Rule: If an attribute X deermines another attribute Y, and Y determines Z, then by transitive nature X determines Z. So it can be written as

   X -> Y, Y-> Z FOLLOWS X-> Z
4. The Decomposition Rule: If there is an attribute X that determines 2 attributes Y and Z, then they can be written as 2 different functional dependencies as X determines Y and Y determines Z or in other words it can be written as

   X -> YZ FOLLOWS X -> Y, X -> Z
5. The Union Rule: If there are 2 separate functional dependencies that an attribute X determines Y and the same attribute X determines Z then they can be combined together into a single functional dependency that X determines both Y and Z and this can be written as

   X ->Y , X -> Z FOLLOWS X -> YZ

6. The Psuedotransitive Rule: Thepsuedotransitive rule can be found out by combining the properties of Transitive Rule and Augmentation Rule.

   If suppose it is given to us that X -> Y 1

   and it is also given that WY -> Z 2

Then if we augment W in the 1st functional dependency, it becomes

WX -> WY 3

From functional dependency 3 and functional dependency 2 it follows

WX -> WY

WY -> Z

So WX -> Z, from the transiive nature.

Therefore PsuedoTranssitivity means that if it is given to us that X -> Y and WY -> Z then it follows WX -> Z.

The inference rules 1, 2 and 3 re known as Armstrong's inference rules or Armstrong's Axioms.

These inference rules have the speciality that they can infer new functional dependencies or new facts.

We also say that inference rules 1, 2, and 3 are sound and comlete.

By sound we mean that if we have a set of functional dependencies F which are given for a relation R, any functional dependency that is inferred from F using inference rules 1, 2 or 3 holds in every relation state r of R that specifies the dependencies in F.

By complete we mean, by repeatedly inferring functional dependencies using inference rules 1 , 2 and 3 until no more further functional dependencies can be inferred gives us a complete set of all possible dependencies that can be inferred from F.

We use a term Closure for this. The closure of F or {F}+ can be determined from F by using inference rules 1, 2 and 3 and these 3 rules are sufficient to get the closure of F.

5.3.2 Closure of Functional Dependencies

To find the closure of a set of functional depepndencies given in F we use the following algorithm or psuedocode.

Let a be a set of attributes, we want to find out the closure of a denoted by α^+ .

The set α^+ consists of all functional dependencies logically implied by a.

The input to the algorithm is given as a set of attributes stored in a and the output is given in the variable result.

```
begin
    result = α ;
    while (changes to result) do
    for each F.D β -> γ in F do
        begin
            if β is a subset of result then
                        result: = result U γ
            end
    end while
    {a+} = result
end
```

here β -> γ is each functional dependency hat is specified in F, where β represents the attributes on left hand side of the F.D. which functionally determine the attributes represented by γ.

The algorithm is simple, we first put the attributes whose closure is to be found (given in α) in the result variable. Then we take each F.D. of F as β -> γ and in that F.D. if β is a subset of the result we include the γ in the result.

This continues till all the FDs have been examined and there are no more changes to the result.

Then finally the result is declared as the closure of a which is denoted by α^+ .

To explain with the example, let us take the following relation R with attributes.

R = {A, B, C, G, H, I } and the following functional dependencies are specified in F.

A -> B

A -> C

CG -> H

CG ->I

B -> H

We take the attributes AG equal to a or in other words we wnt to find the closure of attributes AG denoted by {AG}+.

So a = AG is input to the algorithm.

So in the first step we put into the variable result the value of a.

So result = AG

1st time we execute the while loop, we take the F.D. A -> B as β -> γ. So in other words β = A and γ = B.

Since A is a subset of the result i.e. (AG) , γ. (which is B) is included in the result , so result becomes { A, G, B,}

2nd time the while loop executes with Functional Dependency A -> C

β = A and γ = C.

Since A is a subset of the result i.e. (AGB) , γ. (which is C) is included in the result , so result becomes { A, G, B, C }.

3rd time the while loop executes with Functional Dependency CG -> H

β = CG and γ = H.

Since CG is a subset of the result i.e. (AGBC) , ?. (which is H) is included in the result , so result becomes { A, G, B, C, H }.

4th time the while loop executes with Functional Dependency CG -> I

β = CG and γ = I.

Since CG is a subset of the result i.e. (AGBCH) , γ. (which is I) is included in the result , so result becomes { A, G, B, C, H, I }.

5th time the while loop executes with Functional Dependency B -> H

But no changes are made to the result since H is already included in the result.

So the algorithm terminates.

So the result is now assigned to the closure of a. $\{\alpha\}+$

So in this case a was AG.

So it can be writen as

$\{AG\}^+ = \{ A, B, C, G, H, I \}$

These types of closures also help in computing the key of a relation. So here for the relation R = { A, B, C, G, H, I }

Since closure of AG determines all the attributes present in the relation R. so AG can become the key of the relation R.

5.3.3 Equivalence of sets of Functional Dependencies

Let us first define what is the meaning of the equivalence of sets of functionall dependencies.

A set of functional depepndencies F is said to cover another set of functional dependencies E if every FD in E is also covered in F.

In other words if every dependency in E can be inferred by F and also every dependency in F can be inferred by E. Then they are said to be equivalent.

Two sets of functional dependencies E and F are equivalent if $\{E\}^+ = \{F\}^+$

Or we can say that equivalence exists if E covers F and F covers E.

Let us take an example to explain this:

Suppose F = { A -> C, AC ->D, E -> AD, E -> H }

G = { A -> CD, E -> AH}

To show equivalence, we prove that G is covered by F and F is covered by G.

G will be covered by F, if closure of F covers all functional dependencies of G. and

F will be covered by G, if closure of G covers all functional dependencies of F.

Proof that G is covered by F.

Finding Closure of F and showing Functional dependencies of G are covered.

$\{ A \}^+ = \{ A, C, D \}$ which covers A -> CD in G

$\{ E \}^+ = \{ E, A, D, H, C \}$ which covers E -> AH in G

Proof that F is covered by G

Finding Closure of G and showing Functional dependencies of F are covered.

$\{ A \}^+ = \{ A, C, D \}$ which covers A -> C in F

$\{ AC \}^+ = \{ A, C, D \}$ which covers AC -> D in F

$\{ E \}^+ = \{ E, A, D, H, C \}$ which covers E -> AD, E -> H in F.

5.3.4 Minimal sets of Functional Dependencies

A minimal cover of a set of functional dependencies E is the set of functional dependencies F, which ensure that every dependency in E is in the closure of F or $\{F\}^+$.

And also if we remove any dependency from the set F then the minimal cover stops to exist.

The minimal cover is also known as the canonical cover and it has no dependencies.

We can also state the above in other words as follows.

A canonical cover of F is a minimal set of functional dependencies equivalent to F having no redundant dependencies or redundant parts of dependencies.

For example,

A -> C is redundant in

A -> B, B-> C, A -> C

There are two types of redundancies that can exist.

(1) One is of the Right Hand Side (RHS)

(2) One is of the Left Hand Side (LHS)

Example of RHS

A -> B, B -> C, A -> CD

Can be simplified as

A -> B, B -> C, A -> D

Because A ->C in the 3rd dependency is obvious from the transitive nature of 1st and 2nd dependency.

Example of LHS

A -> B, B ->C , AC -> D

Can be simplified as

A -> B, B -> C, A -> D

Because A -> C is obvious from the 1st and 2nd dependencies.

So when A is determining C then C can be removed from AC -> D and A alone is sufficient to determine D.

To find the minimal cover, it is said to follow these rules :

(1) Remove all trivial FDs

(2) Repeatedly apply the following;

(a) Uniion Simplification.

(b) RHS simplification

(c) LHS simplification

The result you will get will be the minimal cover.

To show how we can get te minimal cover we take an example.

Suppose the following set of functional dependenciess are given:

1. E -> G
2. G -> S
3. E -> S

Using the union rule we combine FDs 1 and 3 and get

1. E -> GS
2. G -> S

By simplifying the RHS of FD 1 we get

E -> G

G -> S

So thi is the minimal cover as well as the canonical cover. So in other words minimal cover and canonical cover is the same.

Let us take another exmple to solve the minimal cover.

R = { A, B, C}

F = {

1. A -> BC
2. B -> C
3. A -> B
4. A, B -> C }

FD 3 is trivial because it is already covered in FD1.

So we are left with

1. A -> BC
2. B -> C
3. A, B -> C

We remove the extraneous atribute on the RHS of FD 1.

A -> BC

B-> C

So A -> C is implie and C is the extraneous atribute so we remove it.

So now we are left with

1. A -> B
2. B -> C
3. A, B -> C

From FD1 and FD2 , we have A -> B and B -> C

So B is extra in the LHS of A, B -> C

So removing B from FD 3, we are left with

A -> B

B -> C

A -> C

As A -> C is impllied from the transitive nature of 1st two depepndencies and therefore the answer is

A ->B and

A -> C

5.4 NORMAL FORMS

Now that we have learnt the concepts of functional dependencies, we are in a place to show their use in putting the attributes in proper tables through the process of Normalization.

The normalization proces is based on taking the relational schema through a series of tests to prove that it satisfies some normal forms.

In normalization, the tabless which do not satisfy the conditions given in normal forms are decomposed into smaller relation schemas that meet the conditions of normal forms and hence have the properties of being non-redundant and minimizing insertion, deletion and uppdationanamolies.

The basic normal forms as discussed earlier are 1st , 2nd and 3rd Normal Forms and after that comes BCNF and 4th and 5th Normal forms. Also two more properies should be satisfied in completing the whole process of Normalization.

(1) The lossless join decomposition property which ensures that no wrong tuples are generated and will be discussed later.

(2) The dependency preservation property which makes sure that each functional dependency is repreented in some individual relation or tablee after decomposing.

Here we need to discuss the concepta of Keys again.

The key is an attribute or a set of atributes which identify a tuple uniquely from the table.

A key K is the superkey with the additional property that removal of any attribute from K will cause K not o be a superkeyany more.

The difference between a key and a superkey is that the key has to be minimal.

If a relation which has more than one key, then all keys become candidate keys.

One of the candidate key is choosen to become the primary key and on the primary key the index for searches is created, when searches have to be made on the database.

The attributers of a relation which form the key (Primary or Candidate) are called the prime atributes.

Those attributes which do not form the key (primary or candidate) are called as non – prime attributes.

For exmple, in the relation

STUDYING. (Student_id, Course_id , grade)

The course_id and Student_id are the prime attributes and the grade is the non-prime attribute.

5.4.1 First Normal Form

The first normal form states that the domain of an attribute must have only atomic values and that the value of any attribute in a tuple must be a single value from the domain of that attribute.

We can also say that First Normal Form discourages multivalued attributes or composite attributes and therefore the relations need to be decomposed so that single values can exist in each cell.

For Example, Take the relation

SUPPLIER(Supplier_id, Supplier_name, Supplier_location)

Suppose we have the following snapshot of the database or an instance of the databae at any particular given time.

Supplier_Id	**Supplier_Name**	**Supplier_Location**
101	John	Delhi, Bombay, Madras
102	Ajay	Bombay
103	Smith	Delhi
104	Sita	Calcutta, Goa
105	Gita	Poona

Now the suppliers with id 101 and 104 are having multiple values in the Supplier_Location attribute. So we need to make every cell have an atomic value to be in 1st Normal Form.

So the table will become as:

Supplier_Id	**Supplier_Name**	**Supplier_Location**
101	John	Delhi
101	John	Bombay
101	John	Madras
102	Ajay	Bombay
103	Smith	Delhi
104	Sita	Calcutta
104	Sita	Goa
105	Gita	Poona

Now what is the problem with the above table. It has redundant or duplicate information. The name John exists 3 times. The name Gita exists 2 times and it invites inconsistencies. If we have redundant data. So therefore we need to decompose the table into 2 relations.

SUPPLIER

Supplier_Id	Supplier_Name

Where Supplier_Id is the Key

SUPPLIER_LOCATION

Supplier_Id	Supplier_Location

Where Supplier_id and Supplier_Location both form the key, because Supplier_id is not unique and therefore cannot become the key.

But the combination of {Supplier_Id, Supplier_Location}both together determine the unique tuple and therefore both together make the key.

Now if we need to know the name of the suppliers and their cities, we can combine both table SUPPLIER and SUPPLIER_LOCATION on the attribute Supplier_Id and find out. The above tables are in 1st Normal Form because the values are atomic and also no redundancy and inconsistency exists.

5.4.2 Second Normal Form

The Second Normal Form is based on the concept of full functional dependency.

There are two types of dependencies:

(1) Full Functional Dependency

(2) Partial Dependency

Let us describe each one in detail and then we will give the definitionn of Second Normal Form.

5.4.2.1 FULL FUNCTIONAL DEPENDENCY

Suppose let us take the same example of our table STUDYING.

STUDYING(Student_Id, Course_Id, Grade)

We know that the key of this table is { Student_Id, Course_Id }.

We have the following FD

Student_Id, Course_Id -> Grade

Because Grade is determined from which student got what grade in which course. So if we remove one attribute from the LHS of the FD, then that FD stops to exist.

Suppose in Student_Id, Course_Id -> Grade

We remove Student_Id , then

Course_id -> Grade is not possible

because course itself is not sufficient to determine Grade. We should have which student got what grade in which course.

So Course_id cannot deermine Grade.

Similarly if we remove Course_id from the FD

Student_Id, Course_Id -> Grade

Then

Student_Id -> Grade is not possible

Because Student itself is not able to determine Grade, because the Grades are as per the Subject and of which Student.

So Student_Id cannot determine Grade.

So therefore we say that Grade is fully funcionally dependent on Student_Id, Course_id .

Or the FD

Student_Id, Course_Id -> Grade

is a full functional FD, because if we remove any one of the attribute from the LHS the FD ceaes to exist.

We define a funcionl dependency X -> Y a full functional Dependency, if removal of any attribute (say A) from X stops the dependency X -> Y to exist.

Here X = Student Id, Course_Id

Y = Grade

An A = either Course_id or Student_Id

So { X – {A} } -> Y does not hold.

5.4.2.2 PARTIAL DEPENDENCY

On the other hand the partial dependency is that if we have a functional depepndency X -> Y and we remove an attribute (A) from X then the depepndency X -> Y still holds.

i.e.X -> Y

{X – {A} } -> Y still holds.

Let us take an example to explain this.

For example, Consider the table PROFESSOR

PROFESSOR(Id, Name, Dept_id, Salary, Head_Id)

Suppose there is a Functional Dependency

Id, Name -> Salary

Here X = Id, Name

Y = Salary

And if we remove an attribute {A} = Name

{X – {A} } -> Y still holds.

Id, Name -> Salary

Id -> Salary Still Holds.

Because Id alone is sufficient to determine the salary of the professor and Name is not really required.

So here the FD

Id, name -> Salary is partial

That is , if we remove one attribute from the FD.

X ->Y or { X –{A} } -> Y , the dependency still holds.

Now the definition of 2nd normal form is as follows:

2NF: A relation schema R is in 2nd Normal Form, if it is in 1st Normal Form and every non-prime attribute A in R is fully functionally dependent on the primry key of R.

Now to explain the 2NF, let us take an example

Consider the Relation

STUDENT_STUDYING

Student_Id	Course_Id	Grade	Student_Name	Student_Address

Here the Primary Key is {Student_Id, Course_Id}

We have the following FD

Student_Id, Course_Id -> Grade, Student_Name, Student_ Address

The prime attributes are { Student_Id, Course_Id}

The non-prime attributes are { Grade, Student_Name, Student_ Address}

This table is in 1st Normal Form but it is not in 2nd Normal Form.

The non prime attribute Student_Name violates 2NF because it has a partial dependency on the Primary Key of R.

Student_Id, Course_Id ->Student_Name

Also the non-prime attribute Student_Address violates 2NF because it has a partial dependency on the Primary Key of R.

Student_Id, Course_Id ->Student_address

Here

X = Student_Id, Course_Id

A = Course _Id

Y = Student_Address

{ X – {A} } -> Y

Student_Id, Course_Id ->Student_address

We remove the attribute A (Course_Id)

So Student_Id ->Student_Address still holds

Since Student_Id is sufficient to determine the Student_Address

Similarly

Student_Id, Course_Id ->Student_Name

We remove the attribute A (Course_Id)

So Student_Id ->Student_Name still holds

Since Student_Id is sufficient to determine the Student_Name

So both the FDs

Student_Id, Course_Id ->Student_Name

Student_Id, Course_Id ->Student_address are partial

And the FD

Student_Id, Course_Id -> Grade is full functional dependency.

So we need to decompose the table into 2 tables. STUDENT AND STUDYING tables.

STUDENT

Student_Id	Student_Name	Student_Address

STUDYING

Student_Id	Course_Id Grade

In the STUDENT table the Student_Id is the primary key.

And the FD

Student_Id ->Student_Name, Student_Address is fully functionally dependent.

Here the non prime attribute Student_NameStudent_Address are fully functionally dependent on the primary key of R (which is Student_Id)

In the STUDYING table the {Student_Id, Course-Id} is the primary key.

And the FD

Student_Id, Course_Id -> Grade is fully functionally dependent.

Here the non prime attribute Grade is fully functionally dependent on the primary key of R (which is {Student_Id, Course_Id})

5.4.3 Third Normal Form

The Third Normal Form is based on the concept of Transitive Dependency.

A Functional Dependency X-> Y in a relational schema R is transitive dependency if there is a set of attributes Z that is neither a candidate key nor a subset of any key of R and both X -> Z and Z -> Y holds.

For example,

Let us take the table

STUDENT_DEPARTMENT

Student_Id	Student_Name	Student_Address	Dname	Dept_Id

There exists 2 FD s

Student_Id ->Student_Name, Student_Address, Dname, Dept_Id

Dept_Id ->Dname

Here X =Student_Id

Z = Dept_Id

Y = Dname

Here

Student_Id ->Dept_ID so (X -> Z)
Dept_Id ->Dname so (Z -> Y)

And Student_Id ->Dname so (X -> Y)

So all 3 exist and therefore

Student_Id ->Dname is transitive through Dept_Id

Student_Id ->Dept_Id and

Dept-Id ->Dname both are true.

Also the attribute Z in this case Dept_Id is neither a key itself nor a subset of the key.

Definition of 3NF: A relation schema R I in 3NF, if it satisfies 2NF and no non-prime attribute of R is transitively dependent on the primary key.

In the above case, it is not in 3NF because of the transitive dependency of Dname on Student_id through Dept_Id.

So to normalize it, or to make it into 3rd Normal form, we have to decompose the two relations.

STUDENT

Student_Id	Student_Name	Student_Address	Dept_Id

DEPARTMENT

Dept_Id	Dname

In the STUDENT table, student_id is the key and all the non-prime attributes Student_Name, Student_Address and Dept_Id are not transitively dependent on the primary key of R i.e. student_id in this case.

Also the table DEPARTMENT, the Dept_Id is the Key and all non prime attributes Dname are not transitively dependent on the primary key of R i.e. Dept_Id in this case.

The attribute Dept_Id is left in the STUDENT table, because it is the joining attribute of the STUDENT and the DEPARTMENT table. If we want to know the student name and department name he belongs to, we can join both tables STUDENT and DEPARTMENT on the joining Attribute Dept_Id and retrieve the information.

5.4.4. BCNF: Boyce Codd Normal Form

The BCNF is stricter than 3NF. To explain BCNF we have to re-define 2NF and 3NF.

An alternative definition of 2NF is as follows:

2NF:A relation schema R is in 2nd Normal Form if every non-prime attribute A in R is not partially dependent on any key of R.

The difference between the above definition and earlier definition of 2NF is that the earlier definition said (is not partially dependent on the primary key) and this definition is saying (is not partially dependent on any key of R means either primary key or candidate key).

An alternative definition of 3NF is as follows:

3NF: A relation Schema R is in 3rd Normal Form (3NF) if whenever a non-trivial functional dependency X-> A holds in R, either X is a superkey of R or A is a prime attribute of R.

Now to describe BCNF, we have to take the following example schema of sector.

Sector

RealEstate#	Province	Sector#	Size	Rate	State_Tax

There are 2 candidate keys:

RealEstate# and

{province, sector#}

Where RealEstate# is unique across the state and sector# is unique in a province.

We have the following set of functional dependencies in F.

FD1 => RealEstate# -> Province, Sector#, Size, Rate, State_Tax

FD2 => Province, Sector# -> RealEstate#, Size, Rate, State_Tax

FD3 => Province -> State_Tax

FD4 => Size -> Rate

FD3 states that State_tax is determined by a province and does not vary by sector#.

FD4 states that rate of a sector# is determined by its size, regardless of which province it is in.

Now look at FD2 and FD3.

FD2 says province,sector# -> State_tax

FD3 says province -> State_tax

So State_tax is partially dependent on the candidate key { Province, Sector#}

So to make it into 2nd normal form we will have to decompose the table into 2 tables.

Sector 1

RealEstate#	Province	Sector#	Size	Rate

Sector 2

Province	State_Tax

Here in the sector1 table, all the non – prime attributes (size, rate) are fully functionally dependent on the candidate keys (RealEstate# and {province, sector#}).

The prime attributes in this case are RealEstate#, province and sector#. Since they are part of the primary key or candidate key.

And in the sector 2 table. The non – prime attribute State_tax is fully functionally dependent on the primary key of the table which is province.

Now are these tables in 3rd Normal form. Let us reconsider the alternative definition of 3rd normal form. For every functional dependency X -> A, either X should be a superkey or A should be a prime attribute.

Look carefully at Sector 1 Table and FD4.

FD4 states that size -> rate, so in this case niether size is a superkey nor rate is a prime attribute. So therefore the sector 1 table is not in 3rd noral form.

To make it into 3rd normal form, we will have to decompose the table.

So now we make 3 tables:

Sector 1A

RealEstate#	Province	Sector#	Size

Sector 1B

Size	Rate

Sector 2

Province	State_Tax

Now in the above 3 tables X -> A, either X is a superkey or A is a prime attribute.

Consider Sector 1A, size is not a prime attribute but RealEstate# is a superkey and {province, sector# is a superkey}.

In sector 1B, size is a superkey, rate is not a prime attribute.

In sector 2 province is a superkey and State_Tax is not a prime attribute.

So they all satisfy the property of 3rd normal form that X is a superkey.

Now the difference between BCNF and 3NF is that BCNF is stricter than 3NF and says that if there is a functional dependency X -> A , X has to be a superkey, it does not matter whether A is a prime attribute or not.

Whereas in 3NF it says that if there is a functional dependency X -> A , either X is a superkey or A is a prime attribute (any one of the 2 conditions is allowed in 3NF), but in BCNF only 1 condition is allowed and that is that X has to be the superkey.

Now suppose in our 3 tables Sector 1A, Sector 1B, and sector 2, there is another FD that exists as follows:

FD5 => Size -> Province (X -> Y)

Now let us look at our sector 1A table, According to 3NF size is not a superkey but province is a prime attribute so it is in 3NF, but it is not in BCNF which states that X has to be a superkey , so Size has to be a superkey .(here size is a non prime attribute).

So to make it into BCNF we have to decompose the sector 1A table into 2 tables:

Sector 1AA

RealEstate#	Sector#	Size

Sector 1AB

Size	Province

Sector 1B

Size	Rate

Sector 2

Province	State_Tax

Now all the 4 tables above are in BCNF, Because in each table there is a functional dependency X -> A and X is a superkey.

Let us look at the first table sector 1AA RealEstate# -> Size, Sector# (According to FD1)

Here RealEstate# is the superkey.

Now look at Sector 1AB table Size -> Provinnce (Accoring to FD 5) so size is the superkey.

Now in table Sector 1B Size -> rate (According to FD4) so Size is the superkey

Now in Sector 2 table Province -> State_Tax (According to FD3) so province is the superkey.

5.5 Multivalued Dependencies and Fourth Normal Form

Multivalued Dependencies (MVD) occur because of the restriction placed by 1st Normal Form. The first normal form does not allow multiple values to exist in in a single cell and therefore the concept of multivalued dependencies arise. That from a single attribute, it can determine multiple values of another attribute.

A multivalued dependency is denoted by the following notation:

X ->.> Y

It uses a double arrow to indicate that the attribute X multidetermines Y.

Let us take an example,

Suppose we have an employee, and he may have a number of dependents. He may have one wife 2 children, or 1 wife one child etc.

So the employee is given by empid and his dependents are given by dependent name dname. So we write the above FD as

empid ->>dname

when two independent multivalues exist in the same table (Relation). Then the problem arises What that problem is, we will describe in a minute, but first let us see how two independent multivalues exist in one table.

Suppose we have, as told earlier that an employee has multiple dependents so a multivalued dependency exists

empid ->>dname

Also let us assume that the employee has several qualifications. So a multivalued dependency exists

empid ->> qualification

Now both these independent multivalued dependencies exist in the same table as follows:

empid	dname	qualification
101	Sita	B.Tech
101	Gita	MBA

Now the employee 101 has 2 dependents Sita and Gita and has 2 qualifications B.Tech and MBA.

Now the problem that I was referring to earlier is described here in detail. The problem is that in the above table why does Sita occurs with B.Tech and Gita occurs with MBA.

Since these two are independent multivalued dependencies, there is an implicit relationship arising between dname and qualification because in the tuples Sita is occurring with B.Tech and Gita is occurring with MBA.

To remove this implicit relationship, we will have to re-write the table as follows:

empid	dname	qualification
101	Sita	B.Tech
101	Gita	B.Tech
101	Sita	MBA
101	Gita	MBA

So now B.Tech occurs with Sita and Gita both and also MBA occurs with Sita and Gita both.

So the implicit relationship between dname and qualification is removed. But what has arisen, redundancy i.e. duplicate information which may lead to inconsistencies.

Fourth Normal Form

Let us begin with the formal definition of 4th Normal Form (4NF), which states that

- A trivial multivalued dependency does not specify any constraint on R.

Let us again say what is a trivial dependency.

A trivial (or small) dependency must have any one of the following conditions to be true.

X ->> Y is trivial if either

(a) If Y is a subset of X or
(b) X U Y = R (X union of Y gives the relation R itself. In the relation R, X and Y are the only two variables)

A relation schema R is in 4NF with respect to a set of dependencies F if, for every non-trivial multivalued dependency

X ->>Y in F,

X is a superkey for R.

Now let us take the example that we are using of employee

empid	dname	qualification

Now here two independent multivalued Dependencies of type 1:N exist in the same table.

empid ->>dname

empid ->> qualification

Now both these multivalued dependencies are non-trivial, because neither dname is a subset of empid or qualification is a subset of empid and also empid union of qualification does not give the relation R (which has 3 attributes empid, dname, qualification) and also the empid union of dname does not give the relation R(which has 3 attributes empid, dname, qualification).

So we say that both empid ->>dname and empid ->> qualification are non–trivial.

Now if they are non-trivial, then according to 4NF X ->> Y should be the superkey for R. So in other words empid should be the superkey for R.

But if we look at the relation again very carefully we see that the key of the relation is {empid, dname, qualification}, all 3 attributes together combined make up the key of the relation R.

So empid alone is not the superkey and therefore the table is not in 4th Normal Form. To make it into 4th Normal Form, we decompose the table into 2 tables R1 and R2, where we separate the two independent multivalued dependencies. So we have:

R1

empid	dname
101	Sita
101	Gita

R2

empid	qualification
101	B.Tech
101	MBA

Now we take two tables separately. We take table R1 first and see that the multivalued dependency empid ->>dname exists.

Now in this case again the table is not in 4thNormal form because according to 4th Normal Form X->> Y, X should be the superkey. So empid should be the superkey. But again this relation the key is formed by combining both attributes (empid, dname).

But this table R1 is in 4th Normal Form and the trick is that the dependency empid ->>dname is trivial. It is trivial because it satisfies the 2nd property that empid union of dname gives the relation R1. The relation R1 is made of two attributes empid and dname.

So the constraint that empid has to be the superkey was for non trivial MVD and not for trivial ones. So it was mentioned in the definition that a trivial multivalued dependency does not specify any constraint in R in 4NF.

Similarly this can be said for table R2 where

empid ->> qualification

empid must be the superkey of the relation R2. But the key of R2 is made up of both the attributes {empid, qualification}.

But the table is in 4NF according to the reason that the dependency empid ->> qualification is trivial. It is trivial because it satisfies the property empid union of qualification gives the relation R2. The relation R2 is made up of 2 attributes empid and qualification. So therefore R2 is also in 4NF.

5.6 Join Dependency and Fifth Normal Form

A Join Dependency (JD) is said to exist in a relation schema R, that if we decompose the relation schema R into smaller relations as (R1, R2 , ... Rn) and then we take the natural joins of the relation state (r) of all smaller relations (R1, R2, ... Rn) and get back the original Relation state (r) of R. Then a Join Dependency is said to exist in that relation schema or table R.

We represent the above as

$$*(\prod R1\ (r)\ ,\ \prod R2\ (r)\ \ldots\ldots\prod Rn\ (r)) = r$$

Where the * represents the natural join of the tables (R1, R2, ... Rn) and the ∏ R1 (r) denotes the relation state of R at any particular time. The r on the right hand side of the equal to sign represents the relation state r of R (The original table).

Let us demonstrate the above with the help of an example.

Suppose we have a Relation (Teacher-Subject-Student) as R the original relation representing the fact which teacher teaches which subject to which student.

Teacher is represented by the attribute T#

Subject is represented by the attribute J# and

Student is represented by the attribute S#.

Suppose R at any one given time in the database is represented with the following relation state (r) of R.

R

T#	J#	S#
T1	J1	S2
T1	J2	S1
T2	J1	S1
T1	J1	S1

Suppose we decompose the relation R(T#, J#, S#) into 3 smaller relations

R1(T#, J#)

R2(J#, S#)

R3(T#, S#)

Then the relation state (r) of R1, R2 and R3 will be as follows:

R1

T#	J#
T1	J1
T1	J2
T2	J1

R2

J#	S#
J1	S2
J2	S1
J1	S1

R3

T#	S#
T1	S2
T1	S1
T2	S1

Now we take the natural join of R1 and R2. The common attribute between the two tables is J#. so we join tables R1 and R2 on J# and get the following intermediate table. R4.

R4

T#	J#	S#
T1	J1	S2
T2	J1	S2
T1	J2	S1
T1	J1	S1
T2	J1	S1

Let us see how we got the above table.

We take the J# of 1st row of R2 which is J1, now J1 matches the 1st and 3rd row of R1 so we get 1st and 2nd row of R4. Now we take the J# of 2nd row of R2 which is J2, it matches with the 2nd row of R1 and we get the 3rd row of R4. Next we take the J# of 3rd row of R2 which is J1 , and J1 matches 1st and 3rd row of R1 so we get 4th and 5th row of R4.

Now we join the intermediate table R4 with the natural join of the table R3.

The common attributes between R4 and R3 are (T#,S#), so we join R4 and R3 where T# and S# of R3 match the T# and S# of R4 and we get the following table R5.

R5

T#	J#	S#
T1	J1	S2
T1	J2	S1
T1	J1	S1
T2	J1	S1

Let us see how we got the above table.

Let us take 1st row of R3 where T#,S# is T1,S2, so T1, S2 matches 1st row of R4 so we get 1st row of R5. Now we take 2nd row of R3 where T#, S# is T1, S1 and it matches 3rd and 4th row of R4 so we get 2nd and 3rd row of R5. Now let us take the 3rd row of R3, it has T#,S# as T2, S1 which matches 5th row of R4 and we get 4th row of R5.

Now let us compare R5 with the original table R. Both have the same values in each row and the relation state (r) of R is equal to the relation state r of R5. Where R5 have been produced by taking the natural joins of R1, R2 and R3. Therefore we say that a join dependency exists in R.

The definition of 5th Normal form is as follows:

5NF : A relation schema R is in fifth Normal Form, if for every non-trivial Join Dependency JD(R1, R2, R3 .... Rn) in F , every Ri is a superkey in R.

Now if we consider the above example of our Teacher-Subject-Student table (T#,J#,S#). Then the Ris were R1(T#,J#), R2(J#,S#), R3(T#,S#). Now every Ri should be a superkey in R.

The Superkey of R is (T#, J#, S#) and the Ris do not contain all 3 attributes, they have combination of any 2 of them. So there fore the table R(T#,J#,S#) is not in 5th Normal Form.

To make it in 5th Normal form we will decompose it intoR1(T#,J#), R2(J#,S#), R3(T#,S#) tables.

Now look at the 3 independent tables R1(T#, J#) , R2(J#, S#) and R3(T#, S#). They independently are in 5th Normal Form because in them no Join Dependency exists since if we take them individually, they cannot be decomposed and joined back.

For example take table R1(T#, J#). Now if we decompose R1, T# and J# will be separated and there is no common attribute which can join them back together, So therefore no join dependency is existing in table R1 and therefore it is individually in 5th Normal Form. Similar explanation can be given for Table R2 and R3 and they are also in 5th Normal Form.

5.7 Lossless Join Decomposition

When we decompose a relation into a number of smaller relations, then these decompositions must be lossless.

Lossless means there is no loss of any information. Referring to the example used in our discussion of 5th Normal Form, we had a relation (Teacher-Subject-Student) and we decomposed it into 3 smaller relations:

R1 = Teacher – Subject

R2 = Subject-Student

R3 = Teacher-Student

And joined them back on a natural join of * (∏R1 (r), ∏R2 (r), ∏R3 (r)) = r

We got the original relation R with the same relational state (r) of R as was the state before the decomposition.

So this was a lossless join decomposition as there was no loss of information.

Let R be a relation schema, and let F be a set of functional dependencies on R. Let R1 and r2 be two decompositions of R.

To test whether we have made the decompositions lossless or not we need to test the following.

The decompositions will be lossless if at least one of the following is true.

R1 ∩ R2 -> R1

Or

R1 ∩ R2 -> R2

In other words if R1 ∩ R2 gives the relation R1 back or R1 ∩ R2 gives the relation R2 back then the decomposition is said to be lossless.

To explain the above, let us consider the following example,

Let R = (A, B, C, D, E)

We have the following set of dependencies defined on R.

A -> BC

B -> CD

E -> AD

to decompose the above into a lossless join decomposition, we have the 3 relations:

R1 = A, B, C

R2 = B, C, D

R3 = E, A, D

Let us first take R1 and R2

R1 $\cap$ R2 ->B

From the FD

B -> CD by augmentation we will get

B -> BCD

We can say R1 $\cap$ R2 -> BCD (which is R2)

So R1 $\cap$ R2 -> R2 so it is lossless join decomposition.

Let us first take R1 and R3

R1 $\cap$ R3 ->A

From the FD

A -> BC by augmentation we will get

A -> ABC

We can say

R1 $\cap$ R3 ->R1 so it is a lossless join decomposition.

So therefore we can say that the relation

R =(A, B, C, D, E) decomposed into

R1 = A, B, C

R2 = B, C, D

R3 = E, A, D

are all lossless join decompositions.

Let us take another example to explain.

Let R = A, B, C, D, E

R1 = A, B. C

R2 = A, D, E

We have the following set of functional dependencies.

A -> BC

CD -> E

B -> D

E -> A

Now R1 ∩ R2 ->A

A -> BC

A -> ABC which is R1

So R1 ∩ R2 ->R1 therefore it is lossless.

Now let us take another example,

R = empid, empname, proj_no, proj_name, proj_loc, no_of_hours

R1 = emp = empid, empname

R2 = project = proj_no, proj_name, proj_loc

R3 = works = proj_no, empid, no-of_hours

The following set of functional dependencies exist

F = FD1 = empid -> proj_name

FD2 = proj_no -.> proj_name, proj_loc

FD3 = empid, proj_no -> no_of_hours

R1 ∩ R2 -> NIL

R2 ∩ R3 ->proj_no

From FD 2

proj_no -> proj_name, proj_loc

proj_no ->proj-no, proj_name, proj_loc

R2 ∩ R3 ->R2

and

R1 $\cap$ R3 ->empid

From FD1

empid -> proj_name

empid -> empid, proj-name

R1 $\cap$ R3 ->R1

Therefore the decompositions R1, R2 and R3 are lossless join decompositions.

Now let us take an example of a decomposition which is not lossless and which is a lossy decomposition.

Let

R1 = emp-place = { empname , place}

R2 = emp-supply = { empid, supply-id, qty, supply-name, place}

We have the following Functional dependencies:

FD1 = empid -> empname

FD2 = supply-id -> supply-name , place

FD3 = empid , supply-id -> qty

R1 $\cap$ R2 ->place

So we cannot get either of the relation

R1 $\cap$ R2 ->R1 or R1 $\cap$ R2 ->R2

So there fore the decomposition is lossy and there is loss of information.

5.8 Dependency Preservation Property of a Decomposition

The dependency preservation property of a decomposition states that if we have decomposed a relation R into some relations R1, R2……Rn. The functional dependencies that were present in the original relation can be found out from the decompositions or can be inferred from the decompositions.

In other words we want to state that the functional dependencies (FDs) are not lost in between. They are still there and therefore preserved.

To illustrate, let us take the following example,

Suppose there is a relation R(A, B, C, D) and we have the following dependencies (FDs)

A -> B

A -> C

B -> D

Suppose the following sets of decompositions exist:

(a) R1 = A, B, C and

R2 = B, D

Now A -> B is present in R1

A -> C is present in R1 and

B -> D is present in R2

Therefore the dependencies are preserved.

Now suppose we have the following decompositions

(b) R1 = A, B, D

R2 = B. C

Now A -> B is present in R1

A -> C is not present in any relation (either R1 or R2)

and B -> D is also not present in any relation (either R1 or R2)

Therefore the dependencies are not preserved.

Now suppose we have the following decompositions

(c) R1 = A, B, D

R2 = A, C

Now A -> B is present in R1

A -> C is present in R2

And B -> D is present in R1

Therefore again all dependencies can be inferred from either of the two relations R1 or R2 , there fore in this case also the dependencies are preserved.

5.9 Inclusion Dependencies

Inclusion Dependencies are used to specify two types of constraints:

(1) The foreign key or referential Integrity constraint which cannot be described in terms of a functional dependency or multivalued dependency since it has attributes which are present in two differennt Relations or Tables.

(2) The superclass and subclass relationship also cannot be described in terms of a functional dependency or a multivalued dependency or a joiin dependency.

An Inclusion dependency may be described as follows:

A.X < B.Y

Where A and B are Relations aand X and Y are attributes of A and B respectively which specify that at any particular database state a of A an b of B the following is true

Π X (a (A)) is a Subset of Π Y (b (B))

In our examples used in previous chapters of the database, we can have the following inclusion dependencies:

STUDENT_PHONES.STUDENT_ID < PROFESSOR.ID

PROFESSOR.DEPT_ID < DEPARTMENT.DEPT_ID

PROFESSOR.HEAD_ID < PROFESSOR.ID

TEACHING.COURSE_ID < COURSE.COURSE_ID

TEACHING.PROF_ID < PROFESSOR.PROF_ID

STUDYING.STUDENT_ID < STUDENT.STUDENT_ID

STUDYING.COURSE_ID < COURSE.COURSE_ID

These inclusion dependencies represent Refrential Integrity Constraint.

We can also use inclusion dependencies to represent superclass / subclass relationships.

In our example used in previous chapters to describe subclasses and superclasses we can have the following inlusion dependencies:

RESEARCH_SCHOLAR.STUDENT_ID < STUDENT.STUDENT_ID

POST_GRADUATE.STUDENT_ID < STUDENT.STUDENT_ID

UNDER_GRADUATE.STUDENT_ID < STUDENT.STUDENT_ID

Chapter - 6

Transaction Processing

6.1 Introduction

A transaction is a logical unit of work done in its entirety or none at all. The above statement indicates that some logical piece of work has to be carried out, either it should be done properly till the end without any problems, or if problems occur then it should not be completed and stopped then and there hen restarted again.

For example, if we are transferring money from one person's account to another person's account. What we have to do is say debit Rs. 1000 from say account A and credit Rs. 1000 to the account of B. Now the transaction is doing the logical piece of work of deducting Rs. 1000 from account A and crediting Rs 1000 to account B. Now suppose in between when it has deducted Rs. 1000 from account A, then an error occurs and it has not credited Rs. 1000 to account B, then the transaction is not complete. It has deducted the money from one account, the money has been lost in between and the person of account B has not received it since it was not credited to his account. So in this case the transaction has not occurred in its entirety and it should be stopped in the middle, that is it should be aborted and should start again from the beginning. So it should rollback, rollback means that undo the changes that were done, so it should undo the debiting of Rs. 1000 from account A and then restart and occur in its entirety, that is complete it fully till it credits the amount to account B, which it had debited from account A.

6.2 Transaction Concept

The transaction naturally needs its data items to be read and written, so to maintain the integrity of the database, we must follow some rules, which are known as the ACID properties. The acronym ACID stands for:

(1) Atomicity

(2) Consistency

(3) Isolation

(4) Durability

Let us explain the meaning of each property.

(1) Atomicity – The transaction should occur atomically that is all its operations should be carried out till the last operation or if they are disrupted in the middle then none of them should occur.

(2) Consistency - Taking the example of two accounts A and B. Suppose we had Rs. 1000 in account A and Rs. 2000 in account B at the beginning of the transaction and suppose I want to transfer Rs. 100 from account A to account B.

The following set of operations would take place in this transaction.

T_1 : read(A)

A = A -100

write(A)

read (B)

B = B + 100

write(B)

There are two operations in this transaction:

read(P)

write(P)

That is the read (P) operation, reads the value of the variable P and the write (P) operation writes the value of variable P back to the database.

In the transaction T_1, the value of account A is read, then the next statement deducts rs. 100 from the A account, the write(A) statement then writes back the updated value of A to the database. The next statement reads the value of the account of B. Then the next statement adds Rs. 100 to the account of B. Then this updated value of account of B is written back to the database by the write(B) operation.

Now consistency property says that the sum of the values of the account A and account B before the transaction should be equal to the sum of the values of the account A and account B after the transaction.

Now in this case, before the trtansaction account A had Rs. 1000 and account B had Rs. 2000, so the total sum of account A and B was Rs. 3000.

After the transaction the account A had value Rs. 900 and account B had value Rs. 2100, so again the total sum of account A and B was Rs. 3000.

So this is the property of consistency that the sum of both accounts show the same value after and before the transaction when money is transferred from one account to another.

(3) Durability – The Durability property states that once the transaction is complete, the updates done will be saved properly to the disk and will now not change in case an error or system failure occurs.

(4) Isolation –The isolation property ensures that if two transactions are occurring concurrently or at the same time, then they do not give inconsistent values after both transactions complete. They are occurring concurrently but appear to be isolated from each other and this can only happen when they are occurring in a serial fashion. This is achieved by the concurrency control component of the database system.

Let us take an example to understand it properly:

Suppose there are two transactions T_1 and T_2

T_1: read (A)

A = A – 100

write(A)

read (B)

B = B + 100

write (B)

T_2: read (A)

A = A – 200

write (A)

read (B)

B = B + 200

write (B)

Now if these two transactions occur serially that is one after another, then the consistency of the database will be maintained. Either T_1 occurs before T_2 or T_2 occurs before T_1. There will be no interference and no problems will occur. But suppose they are executing concurrently, that is simultaneously both at the same time, so in this case, some portion of T_1 will execute then some portion of T_2, then it will execute some portion of T_1, then T_2 and in this way they will interleave.

So we will be lucky that when T_1 executes it reads the value of A, updates it and writes it back before T_2 reads the value of A. Only then we can have consistency maintained.

This is shown as :

T_1	T_2
read (A)	
A = A – 100	
write (A)	
	read (A)
	A = A – 200
	write (A)

Now suppose we are not lucky and the database system changes the value of A in T_1 but just before it writes back the updated value to database, the database system switches to T_2. Then the consistency of database will not be maintained. This is shown as:

T_1	T_2
read (A)	
A = A -100	
	read(A)
	A = A – 200
	write (A)
write (A)	

In this case transaction T_2 has not read the updated value of A of T_1 because it was not written back and it will show inconsistency. Then in this case isolation is not maintained. To maintain Isolation, the transactions are occurring concurrently but they appear as if they have no interference or dependence on each other's values and updates. They are occurring on their own with the consistency maintained. This is job of the concurrency control manager to see that isolation is done.

6.3 Transaction States

The transaction states describe in what state the transaction is going through. These are the following states of a transaction:

(1) Active

(2) Partially Committed

(3) Failed

(4) Aborted

(5) Committed

(1) In an Active state, the transaction is currently being executed.

(2) The partially committed state is said to arrive when the transaction executes its last statement.

(3) When the transaction is complete and the commit statement is given, then the transaction is said to be committed, in the

committed state, the transaction has successfully made changes to the database on the disk and they can be recovered even if the system failure occurs.

(4) The transaction is said to be failed when it could not complete successfully in between its execution, due to some error or system failure, it could no longer proceed normally.

(5) Aborted, the transaction is said to be in the aborted state, when it failed due to some reason, and now has been restored back to its previous state by rollback. So that all changes which had been made until now have been undone and the transaction is ready to be started all over again for successful completion.

The transaction is considered terminated, either because it was committed successfully or because it was aborted.

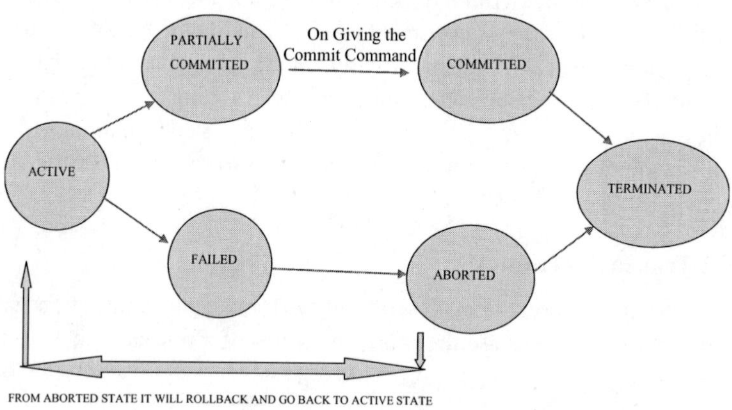

Figure 1.1 The Diagram showing cycle of a Transaction

6.4 Problems that Occur during Concurrency

There are some common problems that occur during concurrency. These are

(1) The Lost Update problem

(2) The Temporary Update (or Dirty Read) Problem

(3) The Incorrect Summary Problem

(1) The Lost Update problem occurs when two transactions are writing to the same data item, but their sequence of operations occurring concurrently becomes such that one transaction will overwrite the data item of other transaction and the value written by the previous transaction will be lost.

For example, consider the two transactions with their sequence of operations occurring as follows:

T_1	T_2
read (A)	
A = A + 100	
	read(A)
	A = A + 200
write(A)	
read (B)	
B = B + 100	
	write (A)
write (B)	

In the above sequence, the item A read in transaction $T_{1,}$ Suppose has a value of Rs. 1000, it has updated its value so A becomes Rs. 1100 but it has not written it to the database. And then transaction T_2 has begun its execution. Transaction T_2 reads the value of A which is Rs. 1000 and adds Rs. 200 to it, now A becomes Rs. 1200. Now transaction T_1 starts executingand writes the value of it's A that is Rs. 1100 to the database. Then it reads the value of another item B and adds Rs. 100 to it. Now transaction T_2 starts executing, it now writes the value of it's A, i.eRs. 1200 to the database.

So the final value of A is Rs. 1200, it has overwritten the value of A of transaction T_1 which was Rs. 1100. So in this case the value of Rs. 1100 was lost for transaction T_1 because T_2 overwrote it by Rs. 1200 and this is the lost update problem.

(2) In the Temporary Update or Dirty Read problem, the data has been updated by a transaction say T_1, it was temporarily written to the database. The new value of that item was read by another

transaction say T_2 and now transaction T_1 has failed and is unable continue.

So in this case, transaction T_2 has read a value of an item in T_1 which was temporary and incorrect, so it is a dirty read.

To understand see the following sequence of events:

T_1	T_2
read (A)	
A = A + 100	
write (A)	
	read (A)
	A = A + 100
	write (A)
read (B)	

——> Transaction T_1 fails
So it should revert back the
value of A to its original value.

In this case suppose A had original value Rs. 1000, it added Rs. 100 to it and A became Rs. 1100, and writes this value of A to the database. Now transaction T_2 has read the value of A as Rs. 1100, it adds Rs. 200 to it and becomes Rs. 1300, it writes this to the database. Now T_1 fails, so it restores back the value of A to Rs. 1000, but T_2 has already read it as Rs. 1100 and this is the incorrect value of A so it is Dirty Read.

(3) In the incorrect summary problem, suppose one transaction is calculating the sum of all the values of the accounts and the other transaction is updating the accounts at the same time. So this will lead to the incorrect sum of all the accounts.

T_1	T_2
	sum = 0
	read (A)
	sum = sum + A

	read (B)
	sum = sum = B
read (C)	
C = C – 100	
write (C)	
	read (C)
	sum = sum + C
	read (D)
	sum = sum + D
read (D)	
D = D + 100	
write (D)	

Now in this above case transaction T_2 is calculating the sum of all the accounts. It adds the values of accounts A and B to the variable sum. Then transaction T_1 starts executing, it reads the value of account of C and wants to transfer Rs. 100 from account C to account D. Now it subtracts Rs. 100 from account C. Now transaction T_2 starts executing, it reads and adds the value of account of C which has deducted Rs. 100 in transaction $T_{1,}$ to the variable sum and also adds the value of account of D to variable sum. Now transaction T_1 starts executing and adds the value of Rs. 100 to account of D. But in this case transaction T_2 has already added the value of account of D to the variable sum and now in transaction T_1 it is updating the value of account of D. So transaction T_2 has read and added the incorrect value of account of D. So the sum of all the accounts will show incorrect value because the amount was subtracted from account of C and that was added to variable sum, but was not added to account of D and D's previous value was added to the variable sum, so this is the incorrect summary problem.

6.5 Schedules and Recoverability

A schedule is a set of operations written in a number of transactions in an order. The operations in the transaction may be read item, write item, commit or abort.

A schedule may use read statements or r and w for read and write with the subscripts as the transaction number.

For example a schedule may be written as:

S

R_1 (X)
W_1 (X)
R_2 (Y)
W_2 (Y)

Where R_1 (X) means a read operation on item X of transaction$T_{1,}$ W_1 (X) means a write operation on item X of transaction $T_{1.}$ R_2 (Y) means a read operation on item Y of transaction T_2 and W_2 (Y) means a write operation on item Y of transaction T_2.

Two operations in a schedule conflict when they satisfy the following 3 conditions simultaneously.

(1) The operations belong to different transactions.
(2) They are performing operations on the same item.
(3) At least one of the operations is a write operation.

Say we have the following schedules:

S_1

T_1	T_2
R_1 (X)	
	W_2 (X)

OR

S_2

T_1	T_2
W_1 (X)	
	R_2 (X)

OR

S_3

T_1	T_2
W_1 (X)	
	W_2 (X)

The above 3 schedules are in conflict because at least one operation is a write operation, they are on the same item X and the operations belong to two different transactions T_1 and T_2.

Suppose we had 2 schedules as follows:

S_4

T_1	T_2
R_1 (X)	
	R_2 (X)

OR

S_5

T_1	T_2
W_1 (X)	
	R_2 (Y)

Then the above two schedules would not have been in a conflict because in S_4 there is no write operation and in S_5 the item is not the same, one is X and one is Y.

6.5.1 Schedules based on Recoverability

Suppose we have the following schedule:

S

T_1	T_2
Read(X)	
Write (X)	
	Read(X)
	Commit
———> fails	
Read(Y)	
Commit	

Here transaction T_2 has performed a read operation on item X and commits itself.

The read operation of T_2 was done when the write operation was performed by T_1 on item X. Thus T_2 has read a value which was updated by transaction T_1.

Now transaction T_2 has committed before T_1 has committed and before T_1 commits, T_1 fails and is aborted and rolled back.

Now since T_2 has read a value that T_1 had written, it should also rollback, but since it has already committed, it cannot be rolled back.

Here is a situation where we cannot recover T_2 from the failure of T_1 and thus this is ***a non recoverable schedule.***

Suppose we had the following situation:

T_1	T_2
Write(Y)	
	Read(Y)
Commit	
	Commit

Here T_2 has read an item written by T_1, and T_1 commits before T_2 commits then this is a ***recoverable schedule***.

6.5.2 Cascading Rollback and Cascadless Schedule

A cascading rollback is a situation in which many rollbacks have to be done together in order to maintain the consistency of the database.

When we say we recover from a schedule , the recoverability will be successful if we are able to start from the point where state of database was same as the original state.

Consider the following Schedule

T_1	T_2	T_3
Read(X)		
Read(Y)		
Write(X)		
	Read(X)	
	Write(X)	
		Read(X)

————> Failure Occurs Here

Now T_1 fails after the Read(X) operation of T_3.

So T_1 needs to roll back, now T_2 has read a value which was written by T_1, so T_2 should also roll back. Now T_3 has read a value which was written by T_2, so T_3 should also roll back.

This is called cascading roll back because one after another the transactions have to roll back because they have read a value which was written by a transaction, which itself is rolling back.

To stop this cascading rollback we have a schedule which is known as cascadless schedule which prevents transaction to be rolled back one after another.

This Schedule states that if a transaction (say T_1) is doing a write operation on an item X then the next transaction (say T_2) which is reading a value of that item X must read it after the 1st transaction (T_1) has performed a commit operation.

Because if a commit is performed then the 1st transaction will not roll back and the 2nd transaction is sure that the value of the item it is reading will not change.

This is shown as below.

T_1	T_2
Write(X)	
Commit;	
	Read(X)

6.6 Schedules and Serializability

Serializability of schedules is concerned with the schedules that are running concurrently. If concurrent transactions in a schedule are conflicting then there is a problem and if concurrent transactions in a schedule are non conflicting then there is no problem.

If the schedules are serial then also there is no problem.

Serial schedules are those in which different transactions occur serially. So no conflicts will be there.

For example,

S1

T_1	T_2
Read(X)	
Write (X)	
.	
.	
.	
	Read(X)
	Write(X)
	.
	.
	.

OR

S2

T_1	T_2
Read (X)	
Write (X)	
.	
.	
.	
	Read (X)
	Write (X)
	.
	.
	.

In the above S2 schedule all operations of transaction T_1 which include read and write statements occur before all the operations of transactions T_2. So there are no conflicts because concurrency is not there. Similarly we can say for schedule S1.

The problem is when schedules are concurrent, i.e. when read and write operations of the transaction T_1 and T_2 of a schedule are interleaved.

For Example,

S1

T_1	T_2
Read (X)	
	Write (X)
	Read (Y)
Read (Y)	
Write (Y)	
	Write (Y)

OR

S2

T_1	T_2
	Read(Y)
Read (X)	
Read (Y)	
Write (Y)	
	Write (Y)
	Read (X)
Write(X)	

In the above in S1 transaction T_1 begins first but T_1 and T_2 are in conflict because there is at least one write statement on same item X. Also true for Y.

Similarly in schedule S_2 transaction T_2 begins first and again has conflict because of at least one write statement on same item Y. Also true for X.

To solve this problem we need to make our concurrent schedules behave like serial schedules.

Because we know that serial schedules will not have any conflicts, so we have our concurrent schedules in which we have to make our operations of both transactions interleave in such a way that there are no conflicts. Then our concurrent schedules are said to be serializable and this is the topic schedules and serializability.

A schedule S is said to be serializable if it is equivalent to some serial schedule.

A schedule is said to be serial if all the operations of all transactions occur one after the other.

If the above is not true then the schedule is non –serial.

Two schedules are said to be conflict equivalent if their conflicting operations occur in the same order in both the schedules, and this has no effect on the result of the database. But if the two schedules have their conflicting operations occur in different order in two schedules, then they effect the result of the database and are not conflict equivalent any more.

Remember the conflicting operations means that there are conflicting instructions where at least one operation is a write operation and it is on the same data item, and belong to different transactions in the schedule.

6.7 Conflict Serializability

Earlier we had discussed that if we make our concurrent schedules behave as serial schedule then there will be no conflicts and they will not affect the result of our database.

To make our concurrent schedules equal to a serial schedule is where the concept of conflict serializability comes.

A schedule is said to be conflict serializable if it is conflict equivalent to a serial schedule.

Two schedules are said to be conflict equivalent if by a series of non conflicting swaps in one schedule we can make it equal to another schedule.

Now what are non conflicting swaps. There are two types of swaps, conflicting swaps and non conflicting swaps.

Conflicting swaps are those in which if we change the order of the operations in two transactions, then it will affect the result of the database. For example,

T_1	T_2
Read(Q)	
	Write(Q)

Here write(Q) occurs in T_2 after read(Q) in T_1, so it has read an item Q from T_1 and now writing it in T_2. So we cannot swap it, swap it means doing write(Q) operation in T_2 before doing read(Q) operation in T_1. i.e.

T_1	T_2
	Write(Q)
Read(Q)	

So in this case T_2 is not reading from T_1 before writing in T_2.

Similarly if we have

T_1	T_2
Write(Q)	
	Read(Q)

Here transaction T_1 is reading a value of Q that transaction T_2 has written, so if we change the order, that is swap it, it will affect the result of the database, that is if we do something like this:

T_1	T_2
	Read(Q)
Write(Q)	

Then T_1 is reading the value of Q before T_2 has written it.

So these are conflicting swaps.

Non conflicting swaps are those in which the change in order does not affect the result of the database.

For Example,

T_1	T_2
Read(Q)	
	Read(Q)

Here if we do a swap or change the order like this

T_1	T_2
	Read(Q)
Read(Q)	

Then it will not affect the result of the database since they are only read instructions and therefore this is a non conflicting swap.

Similarly if we have something like this

T_1	T_2
Write(Q)	
	Write(Q)

And we swap them like this

T_1	T_2
	Write(Q)
Write(Q)	

Then this will not affect the result of the database and it is also a non conflicting swap.

Now let me try to make a schedule S equivalent to another schedule S' by doing non conflicting swaps.

For Example, Suppose we have schedule S.

	T_1	T_2
Op1	Read(P)	
Op2		Write(P)
Op3	Read(P)	
Op4		Read(Q)
Op5	Write(P)	
Op6		Write(Q)
Op7	Read(Q)	
Op8	Write(Q)	

Here Op3 can be swapped with Op4 i.e. Read (P) with Read (Q) because they are non conflicting, since the data item is different.

So it will look like this

	T_1	T_2
Op1		Read(P)
Op2		Write(P)
Op3		Read(Q)
Op4	Read(P)	
Op5	Write(P)	
Op6		Write(Q)
Op7	Read(Q)	
Op8	Write(Q)	

Similarly Op6 can be swapped with both Op4 and Op5 i.e write(Q) with both read (P) and write(P) since again the instructions are non conflicting, since data item is different.

So our final schedule S' looks like this:

	T_1	T_2
Op1		Read(P)
Op2		Write(P)
Op3		Read(Q)
Op6		Write(Q)
Op4	Read(P)	
Op5	Write(P)	
Op4	Read(P)	
Op5	Write(P)	

So now our schedule S and S' are conflict equivalent because we have transformed S into S' by doing non conflicting swaps.

And because S' is equivalent to a serial schedule, we say schedule S is conflict serializable.

6.8 Testing for Conflict Serializability

Whether a schedule is conflict serializable or not can be tested with the help of a precedence graph that can be constructed for each schedule.

If the precedence graph contain a cycle then the schedule is not conflict serializable.

If the precedence graph made for a schedule does not contain a cycle then the said schedule is conflict serializable.

The precedence graph has 2 items:

(1) Vertices

(2) Edges

The vertices represent the transactions in a schedule and the edges represent the order of operations.

Suppose there are 3 transactions in a schedule, then we will have 3 vertices $T_{1,}$ T_2 and T_3 and the edges Ti —>T_j will occur if any one of the following happens:

(1) If a read (X) in Ti happens before a write(X) in Tj then the edge goes from Ti —>$T_{j.}$

(2) If a write(X) in Ti happens before a read(X) in Tj then the edge goes from Ti —>$T_{j.}$

(3) If a write(X) in Ti happens before a write(X) in Tj then the edge goes from Ti —>T_j

S

T_1	T_2	T_3
Read(Q)		
	Write(Q)	
		Write(P)
Read(P)		
	Write(P)	
		Write(P)

The precedence graph of the above schedule S will be made as follows:

For the 3 transactions $T_{1,}$ T_2 and T_3 we have 3 vertices.

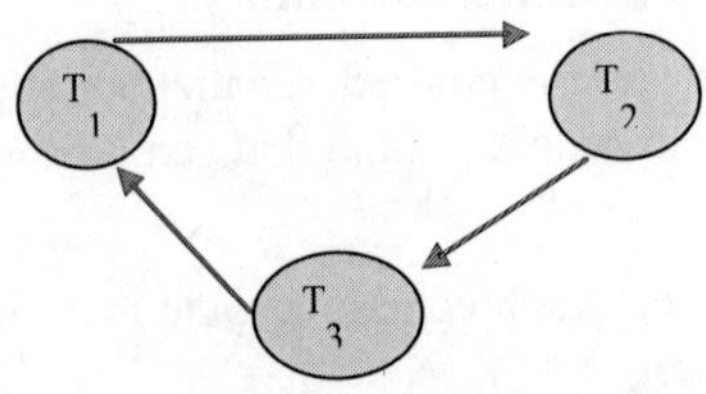

(1) Now read(Q) in T_1 happens before write(Q) in T_2 so the edge goes from T_1 to T_2.
(2) Write(P) in T_3 happens before read(P) in T_1 so the edge goes from T_3 to T_1.
(3) Write(P) in T_2 happens before write(P) in T_3 so the edge goes from T_2 to T_3.

Now a cycle is made for the schedule S so it is not conflict serializable.

Now consider the following schedule S' with 3 transactions T_1, T_2 and T_3.

S'

T_1	T_2	T_3
Read(Q)		
	Read(Q)	
		Write(P)
	Read(P)	
Write(P)		
	Read(P)	
		Read(P)

Three transactions 3 vertices.

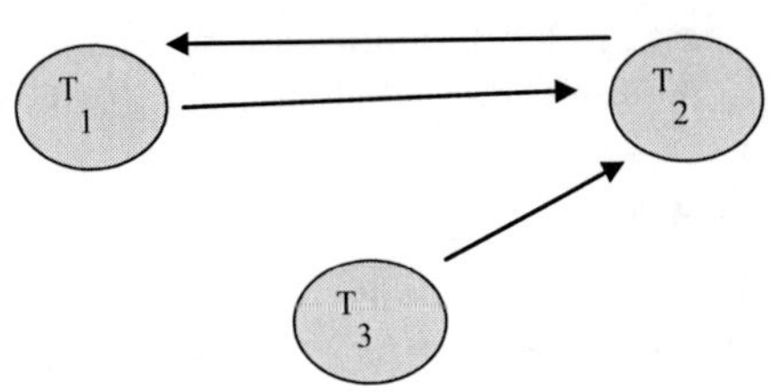

(1) Read(Q) in T_1 happens before Read(Q) in T_2 no edge required.
(2) Write(P) in T_3 happens before read(P) in T_2 so edge goes from T_3 to T_2.
(3) Read(P) in T_2 happens before Write(P) in T_1 so edge goes from T_2 to T_1.
(4) Write(P) in T_1 happens before Read(P) in T_2 so edge goes from T_1 to T_2.

(5) Read(P) in T_2 happens before Read(P) in T_3 so no edge required.

The above graph is also not conflict serializable because it contains cycles.

Consider the following schedule S'' of two transactions T_1 and T_2.

T_1	T_2
Read(P)	
	Write(P)
Write(Q)	
	Write(Q)

Two transactions 2 vertices.

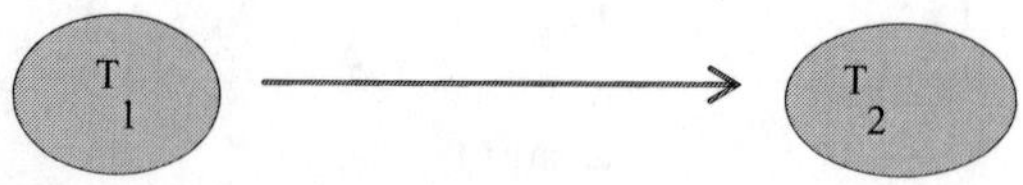

(1) Read(P) in T_1 happens before Write(P) in T_2 so edge goes from T_1 to T_2.

(2) Write(Q) in T_1 happens before Write(Q) in T_2 so edge goes from T_1 to T_2.

So no cycle in the above schedule, therefore it is conflict serializable.

Similarly if there are 3 transactions in a schedule and there are no cycles then again the schedule will be conflict serializable.

6.9 View Serializability

Two schedules are said to be view serializableif they are view equivalent to a serial schedule. The concept of view serializability arises from the fact that both the schedules see the same view of their transactions.

Two schedulers will be view equivalent to each other if all of the following 3 conditions are met simultaneously.

(1) If a transaction say T_1 reads the initial value of a data item in schedule 1, then the same transaction T_1 should read the initial value of that data item in schedule 2 also.

Schedule 1		Schedule 2	
T_1	T_2	T_1	T_2
Read(Q)		Read(Q)	

(2) If the data item say Q is read by a transaction say T_1, which was written by a transaction T_2 in schedule 1, then in the second schedule also the same data item Q should be read by the same transaction T_1 and written by the same transaction T_2.

Schedule 1		Schedule 2	
T_1	T_2	T_1	T_2
	Write(Q)		Write(Q)
Read(Q)		Read(Q)	

(3) If a transaction say T_2 does the final Write of a data item say Q in Schedule 1, then in Schedule 2 also the same transaction T_2 should do the final Write of the same data item Q.

Schedule 1		Schedule 2	
T_1	T_2	T_1	T_2
	Write(Q)		Write(Q)

Suppose there are 3 schedules:

Schedule 1

T_1	T_2
	Read(Q)
	Write(Q)
	Read(P)
	Write(P)
Read(Q)	
Write(Q)	
Read(P)	
Write(P)	

This is a serial Schedule.

Schedule 2

T_1	T_2
Read(Q)	
Write(Q)	
Read(P)	
Write(P)	
	Read(Q)
	Write(Q)
	Read(P)
	Write(P)

Schedule 3

T_1	T_2
	Read(Q)
	Write(Q)
Read(Q)	
Write(Q)	
	Read(P)
	Write(P)
Read(P)	
Write(P)	

Schedule 1 and Schedule 3 are view equivalent because both initial values of Q and P are read in Transaction T_2, final write of P and Q are done by transaction T_1 in both cases. The values read by transaction T_1 of P and Q were both produced by transaction T_2 in both cases.

Since schedule 3 is view equivalent to a serial schedule (schedule 1) therefore it is view serializable.

Schedule 2 and Schedule 1 are not view equivalent because initial value of Q was read in transaction T_2 in schedule 1 and transaction T_1 in schedule 2 (similarly for the value of P)

Also final Write of P and Q was done in Transaction T_1 in schedule 1 and transaction T_2 in schedule 2.

Also the value read by transaction T_1 of P and Q was produced by transaction T_2 in schedule 1 and the value read by transaction T_2 of P and Q was produced by transaction T_1 in schedule 2.

Therefore schedule 1 and schedule 2 are not view equivalent and therefore not view serializable.

6.10 Transaction Support in SQL

The concept of transaction support in SQL deals with the fact that just as transactions in a database occur atomically or does not occur at all, similarly the SQL statements are treated as a transaction. And that SQL statement will occur atomically or will not occur and will be aborted and rolledback if it fails in between and is not able to complete itself.

The SQL statements do not have any begin indication but they do indicate their end and that they do by either giving a commit statement for a successful completion or a rollback statement for an unsuccessful complete.

With each transaction that has to occur in SQL, there is a SET TRANSACTION statement associated with an SQL statement which defines certain characteristics that will be associated with this SQL transaction statement.

There are 3 characteristics that are associated:

(1) Access Mode

(2) Diagnostic Area Size

(3) Isolation Level

(1) The access mode specifies the way in which we are going to access the database. There are 2 modes:

(a) READ ONLY

(b) READ WRITE

The READ WRITE mode allows us to read the database, update it, write on it, insert records into it, delete records from it, create tables, drop tables etc.

The READ ONLY mode allows us to access the database for retrieval of queries.

There is one exception in the data isolation described below, if data isolation is specified as READ uncommitted then READ ONLY mode is assumed otherwise in normal circumstances, the access mode is usually READ WRITE.

(2) The Diagnostic Area Size gives us an integer value specifying the number of conditions that are to be allowed to be applied on the database for the concerned SQL statement. The conditions give an indication of the errors and exceptions that have occurred on the most recently executed SQL statement back to the user.

(3) Isolation Level defines the way in which what types of violations can occur at different levels of Isolation.

There are 4 levels of isolation:

(a) READ UNCOMMITTED

(b) READ COMMITTED

(c) REPEATABLE READ

(d) SERIALIZABLE

Which level is to be used for the SQL statement is given by the ISOLATION LEVEL <value> statement, where <value> is one of the four levels given above.

There are 3 different type of violations which can occur in the database and those are:

(1) Dirty Read

(2) Non Repeatable Read

(3) Phantom

Their detail will be described shortly.

The four levels of Isolation allow different set of violations to occur as per the following chart.

	Type of Violation		
Isolation Level	**Dirty Read**	**Nonrepeatable Read**	**Phantom**
READ UNCOMMITTED	Allowed	Allowed	Allowed
READ COMMITTED	Not Allowed	Allowed	Allowed
REPEATABLE READ	Not Allowed	Not Allowed	Allowed
SERIALIZABLE	Not Allowed	Not Allowed	Not Allowed

Remember this SERIALIZABLE isolation level is different from Serializability.

The default isolation level is SERIALIZABLE, however some systems also allow the READ COMMITTED to become their default isolation level.

Now let us describe each of the violations in detail.

(1) Dirty Read : A transaction T_1which has been written by a transaction $T_{2.}$ T_2does not commit and fails and aborts and is rolledback but now T_1 has read a value which is not correct.

T_1	T_2
	Write(Q)
Read(Q)	
	Not Committed
	Fails
	Aborts
	Rolledback
Incorrect value read By T_1 where $T_2$was not Committed and aborted.	

(2) Non Repeatable read: Suppose transaction T_1 reads a value and later transaction T_2 changes it and then T_1 reads it again. So T_1 has read a different value.

T_1	T_2
Read(Q)	
	Write(Q)
Read(Q)	

(3) Phantoms: A phantom is a row that the transaction sees later then what it had read earlier. For example, T_1 reads a number of rows from a table satisfying some condition and now transaction T_2 inserts a new row which also satisfies the same condition. Now if $T_1$is run again it will see an extra row which was not seen earlier and that is what is called a phantom.

T_1	T_2
Select * From Temporary Where Deptno = '101';	
	Insert Into Temporary Values ('101' ......);
Select * From Temporary Where Deptno = '101';	
Phantom row seen	

Let us take an example to see how the transaction is sup [ported in SQL.

```
EXEC SQL WHEREEVER SQLERROR GOTO REVERSE;
EXEC SQL SET TRANSACTION
    READ WRITE
    DIAGNOSTIC LEVEL 4
    ISOLATIONLEVEL SERIALIZABLE;
EXEC SQL INSERT INTO COURSE (coursename, courseid)
VALUES ('Database Systems', 'CS402');
EXEC SQL UPDATE COURSE
    SET COURSENAME    = 'Database Management System'
    WHERE COURSEOD    = 'CS402';
EXEC SQL COMMIT;
GOTO END_PART;
REVERSE: EXEC SQL ROLLBACK;
END_PART ......;
```

In the above SQL statements we first insert a row in the COURSE table, then we update it, now suppose an error occurs and the SQL statement is unable to continue then the entire transaction will be rolled back and the newly inserted row will also be deleted since by rollback we will undo everything.

6.11 Recovery Techniques

Recovery from a failure can be because of 2 reasons:

(1) There has been a crash in the system.

(2) The database is in an inconsistent state.

When we recover, we bring the database back to the most consistent state in which it was just before the failure point.

In recovery it is important to keep a track of all the changes that have been happening so that at the time of failure, the recovery can be done easily, to do this a system log is kept.

(1) If the failure has occurred due to a disk crash, then in that case, the backup copy which is kept in the archive of the system is picked up, it can be a tape or a disk and the system is brought to the most recent point (consistent state) by copying the contents of the tape on the database. Whenever we take a backup on the tape for recovery process, we ensure that it is in a consistent state.

(2) When the database has not crashed and a failure has occurred due to some transaction failures and the sytem is in an inconsistent state, then it needs to be restored back into a consistent state by undoing some operations and redoing others to bring it back to a consistent state, for that we need our system log.

In this undoing and redoing process, this can further be divided into 2 techniques:

(1) Deferred Update

(2) Immediate Update

(1) In the case of **deferred update**, we have written all the changes to the log and have not written anything to the database. We write to the database when the transaction does its commit operation. Now if the transaction fails before doing a commit, the changes to the database would not have been made. So the database needs no undoing, but we may need to do redoing of the operations, because everything was written on the syatem log, but was not done on the database. So after

the commit, the operations from the system log have to be redone on database.

(2) In the case of **immediate update**, as soon as the changes are recorded on the system log, they are also applied to the database even in the case when the transaction has not done its commit operation. Now if the transaction fails then changes to the database have to be undone and in that case it is called the rollback, and later when the transaction completes successfully the operations from the system log have to be redone to the database.

6.12 Caching

The caching and buffering are normally concepts handled by the operating system. Recovery procedures also use these concepts to enhance the efficiency of the system. In caching the main memory buffers include the data items which need to be updated, they are changed in the cached buffers before writing on the disk.

Recovery can also be done by keeping a set of in memory buffers under the control of a database management system, and this is called the DBMS cache. A directory is associated to know which database items are present in the buffer.

Just like the way a cache works in operating systems, it works here similarly for the DBMS. If a disk page on which update is to be done is first checked in the DBMS cache, if it is present, we need not go to the disk, if it is not present in the DBMS cache, it is fetched from the disk and also put in the DBMS cache, then the changes are made and put back to disk.

Sometimes just as in normal cases, the DBMS cache may be full so an LRU or FIFO technique is used to make space in the DBMS cache. With each buffer entry in the cache, there is a dirty bit kept in the directory entry. When the item is fetched from disk, its dirty bit is set to 0. And when it is modified, it is set to 1. So when the cache is flushed out all entries containing the 1 in the dirty bit are written to the disk.

When the buffers are written to the disk, they can be done in 2 ways:

(1) In Place Updating

(2) Shadowing

In case of **in place updating**, the buffer is written back to the place from where it was picked, so the previous contents are overwritten.

In case of **shadowing,** it writes the updated contents to a different location, so multiple copies are maintained. The old value which had the original value is called the before image and the new value after updation is called the after image. In shadowing, both before image and after image are kept in the disk.

6.13 Database Backup

Database backup is used when we have catastrophic failures in which we may have floods, fire or some other natural disaster or even a disk crash.

To handle from such failure, the recovery manager needs to have a database backup.

The whole database and the system log are copied into a cheap storage medium such as a tape from time to time, so that in any such catastrophic event, we may use that backup to recover the old contents. The backup may be kept at a different geographic location.

Chapter - 7

Distributed Databases

7.1 Distributed Data Storage

A Distributed Databases (DDB) are databases which are interrelated and distributed over a computer network.

A Distributed Database Management System (DDBMS) is a collection of software which manages the database oover the network and does not let the user know how it is doing its work underneath.

The databases in Distributed Databases are stored at different locations indicated by the nodes of the computer network aand their inter relationships are maintained by hyperlinks.

Distributed Databases store the data in the following manner:

The databases are located physically at different geographical locations, which means the Tables, Files, Relations will be located in different locations and their details will be completely hidden from the user.

When a user would give any command, the command would work properly without distinguishin, whether the database is placed at one location or another. For the DDBMS, the command would work normally as if everything is placed at a single location.

The data stored is replicated at many places, so that it is easily available and gives better performance or for backup also. The user does not know whether any such arrangement exist. For him the data is placed at one location and he is working with that.

The storage of data may need to be broken up into parts, so that which ever geographical location needs whatever part. That part is available to it and the rest, which is not needed here, need not be kept here.

So there are 2 different types of fragmentations which are possible:

(1) Horizontal Fragmentation

(2) Vertical Fragmentation

In **Horizontal fragmentation**, the tables or relations are broken row wise. Some of the rows meeting a certain condition are placed at one location and the other rows meeting another condition are placed at another location.

For example, let us take an employee table in which the address is a composite attribute and has city as one of its sub attribute. Now we may like to place the records of an employee who are working in the city 'Delhi' at the Delhi Location (node of the network) and the ones who are working at Bombay will meet the condition City = "Bombay' and place those rows at geographical location (network node) Bombay.

EMPLOYEE

Empid	Name	Dept	Salary	Address	City
101	Amit	IT	20000	Mayur Vihar	Delhi
102	Geeta	CSE	30000	Vasant Kunj	Bombay
103	Deepa	ME	32000	Pali	Bombay
104	Preeti	IT	31000	Chilka	Madras
105	Pawan	EC	27000	Raj Nagar	Madras
106	Parth	EE	33000	Shivalik	Delhi
107	Shivansh	CSE	45000	Pashchim Nagar	Madras
108	Devansh	EC	44000	Pitam Pura	Delhi
109	Kriti	EE	30000	Vasundhara	Delhi

Suppose we have the above table given to us, now we want to do horizontal fragmentation on the attribute city. So it will be fragmented ino 3 tables as follows segregated on cities.:

EMP1

Empid	Name	Dept	Salary	Address	City
101	Amit	IT	20000	Mayur Vihar	Delhi
106	Parth	EE	33000	Shivalik	Delhi
108	Devansh	EC	44000	Pitam Pura	Delhi
109	Kriti	EE	30000	Vasundhara	Delhi

EMP2

Empid	Name	Dept	Salary	Address	City
102	Geeta	CSE	30000	Vasant Kunj	Bombay
103	Deepa	ME	32000	Pali	Bombay

EMP3

Empid	Name	Dept	Salary	Address	City
104	Preeti	IT	31000	Chilka	Madras
105	Pawan	EC	27000	Raj Nagar	Madras
107	Shivansh	CSE	45000	Pashchim Nagar	Madras

The 3 tables broken down can be joined back by merging all the 3 tables back into the original tables without putting any condition.

Vertical Fragmentation

Suppose we have an employee table and that table has details of the employe's personal as well as professional information in the same table. Suppose for any reason we may want to separate the personal information of an employee and the professional information and put them at 2 different geographical locations (nodes of the network)

Asssume we have the following employee table.

EMPLOYEE

Empid	Name	Father _Name	Dept	DOB	Salary	Designation	Address	City
101	Amit	Laxman Singh	IT	12-Jul-1978	20000	Lecturer	Mayur Vihar	Delhi
102	Geeta	Ram Gopal	CSE	15-Aug-1998	30000	Assistant Professsor	Vasant Kunj	Bombay
103	Deepa	Radha Kant	ME	20-Sep-1989	32000	Assistant Professsor	Pali	Bombay
104	Preeti	Krishan Kumar	IT	30-Jun-1988	31000	Assistant Professsor	Chilka	Madras
105	Pawan	Gopal Das	EC	12-Dec-1999	27000	Lecturer	Raj Nagar	Madras

(*Contd...*)

106	Parth	Shyam Sunder	EE	14-Oct-1989	33000	Assistant Professsor	Shivalik	Delhi
107	Shivansh	Vivek Arora	CSE	16-Jul-1998	45000	Associate Professor	Pashchim Nagar	Madras
108	Devansh	Vinay Dhankani	EC	17-Sep-1997	44000	Associate Professor	Pitam Pura	Delhi
109	Kriti	Vijay Dutt	EE	25-Aug-1980	30000	Assistant Professsor	Vasundhara	Delhi

This table will be fragmented into 2 tables as follows:

EMP1

Empid	Name	Father_Name	DOB	Address
101	Amit	Laxman Singh	12-Jul-1978	Mayur Vihar
102	Geeta	Ram Gopal	15-Aug-1998	Vasant Kunj
103	Deepa	Radha Kant	20-Sep-1989	Pali
104	Preeti	Krishan Kumar	30-Jun-1988	Chilka
105	Pawan	Gopal Das	12-Dec-1999	Raj Nagar
106	Parth	Shyam Sunder	14-Oct-1989	Shivalik
107	Shivansh	Vivek Arora	16-Jul-1998	Pashchim Nagar
108	Devansh	Vinay Dhankani	17-Sep-1997	Pitam Pura
109	Kriti	Vijay Dutt	25-Aug-1980	Vasundhara

EMP2

Empid	Dept	Salary	Designation	City
101	IT	20000	Lecturer	Delhi
102	CSE	30000	Assistant Professsor	Bombay
103	ME	32000	Assistant Professsor	Bombay
104	IT	31000	Assistant Professsor	Madras
105	EC	27000	Lecturer	Madras
106	EE	33000	Assistant Professsor	Delhi
107	CSE	45000	Associate Professor	Madras
108	EC	44000	Associate Professor	Delhi
109	EE	30000	Assistant Professsor	Delhi

So the Empid attribute is present in both tables and then they will be joined back on this unique attribute again.

7.2 Concurrency Control in Distributed Databases

In a distributed environment, the following features are included for concurrency.

- Multiple copies of the data items are existing because of replication of databases at different geographical locations. So we need to take care of the fact that all copies of the database at different locations have the same values at any given time. So that there are no inconsistencies.

- If some sites fail to do the commit command, then the two-phase commit protocol is used to deal with this problem.
- Deadlocks may occur at several sites. So techniques for dealing with deadlocks must be brought into practice.

The distributed control technique is based on the concept of a distinguished copt of a data item. The idea is to designate a particular copy of each data item as a distinguished copy. All locking and unlocking requests are sent to that particular site which contains the distinguished copy.

The way in which we choose how to keep distinguished copy is done differently. The following techniques are used:

(a) Primary Site Technique
(b) Primary Site with Backup Site
(c) Primary Copy Technique

(a) In the Primary Site Technique, all distinguished copies are kept at the same one site called the Primary Site.
(b) In the primary Site with Backup Site is another type of Primary Site technique which has a Backup site along with it.
(c) The Primary Copy Technique allows various data items to store their distinguished copy of data items at different sites. A site that contains the distinguished copy of that particular data item acts as the coordinator site so that concurrency technique can be applied on that data item.

Let us look at each one in detail:

(a) The primary site is known to be the coordinator site for all database items. All locks are kept at that site and all the requests for locking and unlocking are sent there. It then follows the two-phase locking protocol.

    Its main disadvantages are:

    (1) All locking requests which are sent to a single site may be overloaded with so many requests and possibly put so much of traffic that the site is unable to handle.

(2) Second, if the site fails then we are stuck and cannot do much until it comes up, because there is no backup.

(b) The second disadvantage is taken care of in the Primary Site with Backup Site option. All locking information is maintained at both the primary and backup sites. In case the primary site fails, the backup site is used to provide the same data.

Because both the primary and backup site need to take care of the granting of locks, acquiring of locks, which in turn slows down the process. Even with this technique both sites can be over loaded with traffic and the problem of bottleneck still remains.

(c) Primary Copy Technique is used to overcome the disadvantage of bottleneck, we put distinguishing copies of data items at different sites. Failure of one site does not affect the data placed at another site.

In case a coordinator site fails. The site that are still running must choose a new coordinator. This may be the case in all the three techniques discussed above. In this case all transactions running may be aborted and restarted.

If a site A, Suppose has to become the new Primary Site and at present A is a Backup Site, then A can choose any of the running sites as Backup Site and it itself (A) can become the new Primary Site.

If in the case of say both Primary and Backup Site are down and we have to choose a new coordinator site. Then say a site B has been communicating with most of the sites and it has been communicating with them for quite some time, then the process of election will take place in which if most sites put a 'yes' in their votes for the site B to become the coordinator site. Then when a minimum number of 'yes' votes are received, B becomes the coordinator site.

Apart from the distinguished data item approach, there is another method which takes place in distributed database concurrency control technique. And that is called the **Method of Voting.**

In this, a lock request is sent to all sites that have the copy of that data item. Each copy maintains its own lock and can grant or deny the requests for it.

If a transaction requests that a lock is to be granted on this data item and a majority of sites agree that yes lock can be granted. Then it locks the data item and informs all sites containing that data item that a lock has been granted.

If that particular transaction which had requested for a lock, did not get a majority and runs out of a certain time period. Then it cancels the lock and informs all sites that it has cancelled that lock.

The method of Voting is considered as the most genuine method of distributed concurrency control because of the reason that all sites are involved in it equally.

But its disadvantage is that it generates a lot of traffic.

7.3 Directory Systems

The directory system of a Distributed Database is just as the directory of people normally known as the yellow pages or the terms given at the end of the book from where you can find which information is placed where.

When directories have to be accessed across distributed databases, they have to follow some directory access protocols such as the LDAP (Light Weight Directory Access Protocol).

Why cannot we use database protocols as simple as ODBC or JDBC. It is simply for the reason that data is kept at different places and may be fragmented also.

Let us discuss the LDAP Protocol.

- The LDAP directory has entries which are similar to objects.
- Each entry must have a unique Distinguished Name (DN)
- And each DN is made up of a sequence of Relative Distinguished Names (RDNs)

  For example, let us take a DN as:

  n = Archana d = IT e= IEC College c = India

where a DN = n = Archana, d= IT, e = IEC College , c = India

RDNs are as follows:

n = name, d=department, e=educational institute, c=country

- The entries can have attributes and attributes are multivalued by default.
- The type of attributes may be of any type. Some Built In are given below:
  (a) Binary
  (b) String
  (c) Time
  (d) Telephone Number
  (e) Address
- LDAP allows definition of Object Classes.
- The Object Classes will have attribute names and types.
- The object classes may use inheritance to define object classes.
- The entries can have one or more Object Classes.

The entries are organized into a Directory Information Tree according to their DNs.

(a) The leafs represent specific objects.
(b) The internal nodes represent RDNs
(c) Children of a node inherit the DN of the parent and can have their own RDNs also.
(d) The DN of an entry can be found out by traversing the path from the root.

Chapter - 8

Concurrency Control

8.1 Concurrency Control

Concurrency Control means that when we have two or more transactions which occur concurrently then we must ensure the Isolation Property of the transactions and also ensure Conflict Serializability to ensure that the database system remains consistent.

There are a number of techniques by which we can ensure that concurrency control is taken care of . These techniques are:

(1) Locking of data items

(2) Timestamp Based

(3) Validation Based

(4) Granularity of Data Items

(5) Graph Based Protocol.

The simplest way to ensure that the transactions do not conflict and may be able to run simultaneously or parallel or concurrently is by locking. Now here simultaneously or parallel does not mean that we are taking about multiprocessing systems or more than 1 CPU. This means that there is only one database management system and it ensures that the transactions are interleaved to run one after another but at a single point of time only one operation of any one of the transactions will take place.

Locking is a method in which we ensure locks on the data items. There are a number of locks available. Normally there are shared locks and exclusive locks. Shared locks should be applied on a data item when that data item has to be read. Exclusive locks should be applied on a data item when that data item needs to be updated.

Basically the shared mode of locks allows many transactions to read the same data item and they can all lock the data items in their transactions in shared mode.

Exclusive mode of lock will allow only one transaction to lock a data item in exclusive mode so that a write operation can be performed on that data item. But it does not allow any other transaction to lock that data item in shared or exclusive mode in their transactions.

There is a compatibility matrix of shared and exclusive locks of say two transactions T_1 and T_2.

		T_1	
		Shared	**Exclusive**
T_2.	**Shared**	True	False
	Exclusive	False	False

The above matrix clearly says that if a transaction T_1 has applied a shared lock on a data item say X and transaction T_2 is also trying to lock the same data item X in shared mode then it is allowed so the value of True in the matrix. (That is both only want to read data item X). Now if transaction T_1 applies an exclusive mode lock on a data item say X in its transaction and another transaction T_2 wants to apply a shared lock on the same data item in its transaction, then that is not allowed and is shown by a false value in the matrix. Here the transaction T_1 has applied exclusive lock on X for writing onto X and T_2 wants to read it (because it is applying a shared lock) then it is not allowed. Similarly if T_2 has already applied for an exclusive lock on X and now T_1 wants to apply for a shared lock on X, then again it is not allowed and shown by a false value. Now if both transactions want to write on it and T_1 has already applied an exclusive lock on a data item X, now T_2 also wants to write on X and also is trying to apply an exclusive lock on X, then again that is not allowed and indicated by a false value in the matrix.

8.2 Guaranteeing Serializability with the help of Locks

There are a number of protocols which can be used to ensure serializability with the help of locking techniques.

They are discussed as follows:

8.3 The Two-Phase Locking Protocol

In the two phase locking protocol there are 2 phases:

(1) The growing Phase

(2) The shrinking Phase

In the growing phase, all locks can be acquired, for example all shared locks or exclusive locks can be granted in this phase.

In the shrinking phase all locks can be released, i.e unlocked. For example all shared and exclusive locks can be unlocked.

The protocol says that:

(1) The growing phase happens before the shrinking phase.

(2) Once the growing phase is over and the shrinking phase strated, we cannot get back to the growing phase again.

In other words, we lock all the data items first (in the growing phase). Once we have locked all the data items and we start releasing the data items (in the shrinking phase) then we cannot lock further items or the items locked before.

Let us take the following schedule as an example:

T_1	T_2
LOCK_S(X)	LOCK_S(Y)
READ(X)	READ(Y)
UNLOCK(X)	UNLOCK(Y)
LOCK_X(Y)	LOCK_X(X)
WRITE(Y)	WRITE(X)
UNLOCK(Y)	UNLOCK(X)

The LOCK_S notation is used for a shared lock and LOCK_X notation is used for an exclusive lock.

If we say LOCK_S(X), that means I am locking the data item X in Shared mode and if I use LOCK_X(X), that means I am locking the data item X in exclusive mode.

The above schedule does not follow the Two Phase Locking Protocol because it acquires a lock (LOCK_S(X)) and then releases a lock (UNLOCK(X)), then again acquires a lock (LOCK_X(Y)) and then again releases a lock (UNLOCK(Y)).

Now if we want to make it follow a two phase locking protocol, then all locks should be acquired first, and once the unlocking starts, then no more locks can be acquired.

T_1	T_2
LOCK_S(X)	LOCK_S(Y)
READ(X)	READ(Y)
LOCK_X(Y)	LOCK_X(X)
WRITE(Y)	WRITE(X)
UNLOCK(X)	UNLOCK(Y)
UNLOCK(Y)	UNLOCK(X)

So this schedule given above now follows the two phase locking protocol.

The two phase locking technique just discussed is called the basic two phase locking. There are a number of variations of two phase locking and they are:

(1) Strict two phase locking

(2) Rigorous two phase locking

The two phase locking protocol ensures conflict serializability but it cannot ensure that deadlock will not occur.

For example, if the above schedule occurs concurrently as follows then it will be deadlocked.

T_1	T_2
LOCK_S(X)	
READ(X)	
	LOCK_S(Y)
	READ(Y)
	LOCK_X(X)
	WRITE(X)
LOCK_X(Y)	
WRITE(Y)	

Now in transaction T_1, X is locked in shared mode, then in transaction T_2, Y is locked in shared mode, then transaction T_2 is trying to lock X in exclusive mode, but since a shared lock already exists on X it will not be able to proceed, but T_1 is trying to lock Y in exclusive mode and since Y is already locked in shared mode, it will not be able to lock Y in exclusive mode. So both transactions T_1 and T_2 wait for each other to proceed, but since all unlocks appear at the end, no transaction will reach the point where unlocking of X or Y is done and they will be deadlocked.

8.4 Strict Two-Phase Locking Protocol

The strict two phase locking protocol ensures that a cascading rollback will not occur because in two phase locking protocol a cascading rollback can occur.

For example, Consider the following schedule:

T_1	T_2	T_3
LOCK_X(P)		
READ(P)		
LOCK_S(Q)		
READ(Q)		
WRITE(P)		
UNLOCK(P)		

	LOCK_X(P)	
	READ(P)	
	WRITE(P)	
	UNLOCK(P)	
		LOCK_S(P)
		READ(P)

⟶ Failure of T_3 occurs here

Now the above schedule follows two phase locking protocol, but if T_3 fails, then it will rollback and it will cause T_2 to rollback also, since the value of P read by T_3 was produced by T_2. Now T_2 will cause T_1 to rollback, since the value of P read in T_2 was produced by T_1 so this is a cascading rollback.

Now in strict two phase locking protocol, it ensures that a cascading rollback will not occur and the protocol commits the transaction before unlocking the data item.

So the above schedule will appear as follows:

T_1	T_2	T_3
LOCK_X(P)		
READ(P)		
LOCK_S(Q)		
READ(Q)		
WRITE(P)		
Commit;		
UNLOCK(P)		
	LOCK_X(P)	
	READ(P)	
	WRITE(P)	
	Commit;	
	UNLOCK(P)	
		LOCK_S(P)
		READ(P)

Another variation of two phase locking protocol is the rigorous two phase locking protocol.

8.5 Rigorous Two-Phase Locking Protocol

The difference between strict two phase locking protocol and rigorous two phase locking protocol is that in strict two phase locking it holds all the exclusive locks until the transaction commits and then unlocks the exclusive locks, whereas in rigorous it will hold all locks whether they are shared or exclusive until the transaction commits and only then it will unlock all locks whether shared or exclusive.

8.6 Deadlock Free Protocols

The two phase locking protocols discussed above are not free from deadlock. Now we discuss the protocols which are free from deadlock and they are:

(1) Graph Based Protocol

(2) Timestamp Based Protocol

(3) Validation Based Protocol

(4) Multiple Granularity Based Protocol

Let us discuss each one of them:

8.7 Graph Based Protocol

The graph based protocol has a pre-requisite that we must know in advance that which of the data items will be accessed in which order.

This protocol also ensures conflict serializability. If we have a set D = { d1, d2……dn}, where d1, d2 etc are data items. If an edge goes from di -> dj, it means that the data item di must be accessed before accessing the data item dj.

This partial ordering of data items must be known before and they may come from a logical organization of the data.

Due to this partial ordering, we can make a directed acyclic graph of all the data items in set D, and this is also known as a database graph.

The graph based protocol may be viewed as a tree protocol which may be considered as a variation of it.

8.7.1 Tree Protocol

In the tree protocol only exclusive locks are allowed and they may be denoted as LOCK_X.

The tree protocol obeys the following rules:

(1) A data item can be locked by each transaction say T_i at most once

(2) The transaction T_i may obtain its first lock on any data item.

(3) Later on, a data item Z may be locked by a transaction T_i only if the transaction T_i has already locked the parent of Z.

(4) The unlocking of data item may take place at any time.

(5) Once a data item has been locked and unlocked by $T_{i,}$ it cannot be later on relocked by T_i again.

The schedule that follow the tree protocol rules ensure conflict serializability.

Let us take an example to demonstrate the tree protocol.

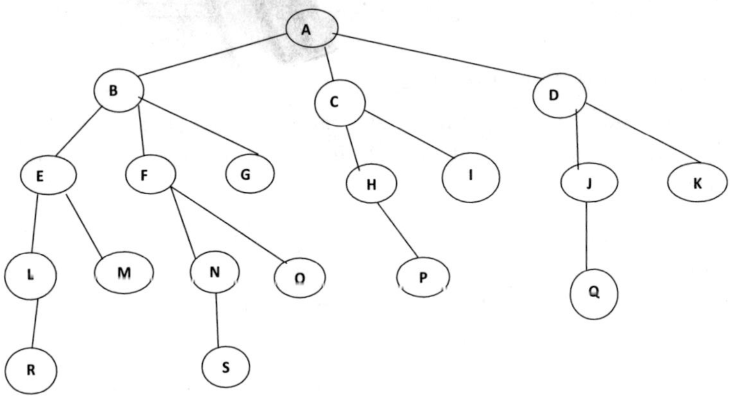

Let us assume that the following four instructions take place:

T_1 : LOCK_X(C); LOCK_X(H); LOCK_X(I); UNLOCK(C); UNLOCK(I); LOCK_X(P); UNLOCK (H); UNLOCK (P);

T_2 : LOCK_X(B); LOCK_X(E); UNLOCK(B); UNLOCK(E);

T_3 : LOCK_X(C); LOCK_X(I); UNLOCK(I); UNLOCK(C);

T_4 : LOCK_X(B); LOCK_X(F); UNLOCK(B); UNLOCK(F);

Let the transactions follow the following schedule:

T_1	T_2	T_3	T_4
LOCK_X(C)			
	LOCK_X(B)		
	LOCK_X(E)		
	UNLOCK (B)		
LOCK_X(H)			
LOCK_X(I)			
UNLOCK(C)			
UNLOCK (I)			
			LOCK_X(B)
			LOCK_X(F)
		LOCK_X(C)	
		LOCK_X (I)	
	UNLOCK(E)		
LOCK_X(P)			
UNLOCK(H)			
		UNLOCK(I)	
		UNLOCK (C)	
			UNLOCK (B)
			UNLOCK (E)
UNLOCK(P)			

Observe that when there is a LOCK_X on data item B in transaction $T_{2,}$ no other transaction can lock B, once transaction T_2 unlocks B, then transaction T_4 locks B. Note transaction T_1 holds locks on two disjoint subtrees H and I.

Now this schedule is not only conflict serializable, but it is also free from deadlock since the graph does not make a cycle. It is an acyclic graph.

This schedule is not recoverable an does not ensure cascadelessness. To make it a cascadeless schedule, we should ensure that all locks are released at the end, but then it will reduce concurrency.

The advantages of this protocol are:

(1) The main advantage of a tree protocol over two phase locking protocol is that it is free from deadlock.

(2) Another advantage is that unlocking of data items may take place at any time so the concurrency is increased and the waiting time for data item is reduced.

The disadvantages of this protocol are:

(1) The prior knowledge of what needs to be accessed in which order is difficult to implement, they may lock the root of the tree which will reduce concurrency.

(2) Also the protocol unnecessarily locks data items, which need not to be locked. For example, in the above schedule, suppose it needs to access H and I, but it also locks C.

This additional locking results in the overhead being increased for locking and the waiting time may be larger which may result in decrease in concurrency.

8.8 Timestamp Based Protocol

The two phase locking protocol guarantees conflict serializability schedules but the only problem is that if it locks an item, that item cannot be used by another transaction until it is unlocked.

The timestamp based protocols follow a different way of solving the problem, ensuring conflict serializability without locking. Here they use a timestamps and a timestamp ordering protocol lays down its rules, those transactions which follow the rules ensure conflict serializability.

First let us define the term timestamp, a timestamp is a value of the current time, which may be taken from a system clock or a counter, just to indicate the order in which the transaction arrived early and which was late in relation to each other.

The timestamp ordering protocol does not use any locks, so there is no question that a deadlock will occur and hence the protocol is free from deadlock situation.

Let us note down the type of timestamps that we are going to use in our timestamp ordering protocol.

(1) $TS(T_i)$ – A unique fixed timestamp associated with the transaction $T_{i,}$ indicating the time before T_i begins its execution. This is assigned by the database system itself.

(2) R_Timestamp(Q) - Gives the time of the latest read of the item Q done by any transaction. For example, if there are 2 transactions T_i and T_j and the order of operations occurs as follows:

T_i	T_j
	Read(Q)
Read (Q)	

Then the latest read of item Q was done by transaction T_i in that case. The value that R_Timestamp(Q) gets the value of time when Read(Q) occurred in transaction T_i and not when Read(Q) occurred in transaction $T_{j.}$

(3) W_Timestamp(Q) – Gives the time of the latest write of the item Q done by any other Transaction. For example, if there are 2 transactions T_i and T_j and the order of operations occurs as follows:

T_i	T_j
Write(Q)	
	Write (Q)

Then the latest write of item Q was done by transaction $T_{j,}$ in that case the value that W_Timestamp(Q) gets the value of the time when Write(Q) occurred in T_j and not when Write(Q) occurred in transaction T_i.

8.8.1 The Timestamp Ordering Protocol

The purpose of having a timestamp ordering protocol is to make sure that if there are any Read or Write conflict operations, then they are executed in the manner that the timestamp ordering protocol has decided.

These are the ways in which the protocol operates:

(1) Let a transaction T_i issue a Read(Q) operation

(a) If $TS(T_i)$ < W_Timestamp(Q)

That means the start of transaction T_i has happened before the latest write operation on data item(Q), Now T_i wants to read a data item (Q), but another transaction in between performs a Write(Q) operation before T_i got a chance to read it. So the transaction is rejected and T_i is rolled back.

Pictorially we can say the operation executed as follows:

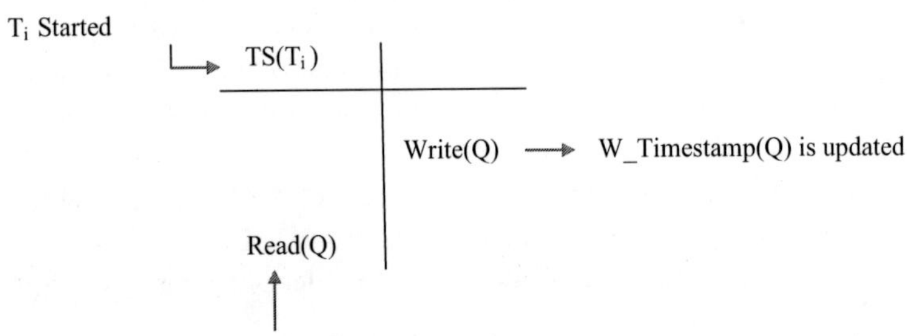

T_i started to Read(Q) but a Write(Q) happened before it and therefore T_i is not reading the correct value that it was supposed to when it started, therefore reject and rollback.

(b) If $TS(T_i)$ >= W_Timestamp(Q)

That is if the transaction T_i started after the latest write operation on data item(Q) has taken place, and then you want to issue a Read(Q) operation. So there is no problem. The Read(Q) operation is reading the correct updated value, so let the transaction take place.

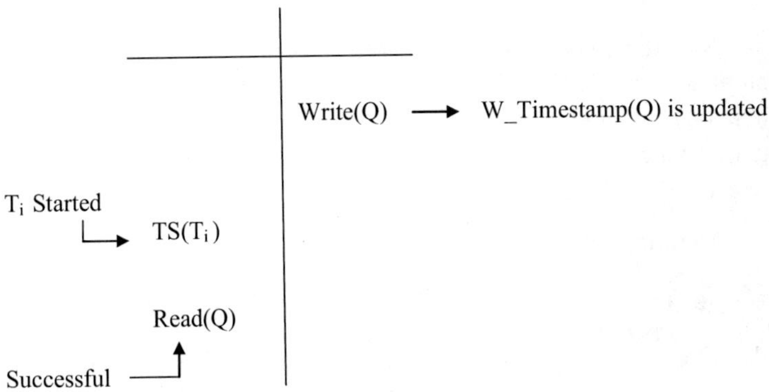

2. In the second case, now suppose a transaction wants to issue a Write(Q) operation.

(a) If $TS(T_i) < R\_Timestamp(Q)$

Now the transaction T_i has started, and a read operation on data item (Q) takes place by another transaction before T_i gets a chance to perform a write operation on data item (Q), for which it had started. So again another transaction has read a value of Q before T_i got a chance to write it, so again reject and rollback.

Pictorially if we see the operations execute in the following manner:

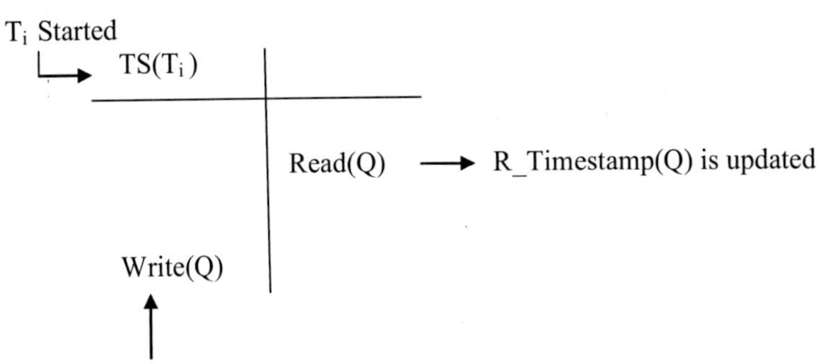

Write(Q) occurring after Read(Q), so Read(Q) has not read the proper value, so reject and rollback.

(b) If $TS(T_i) < W\_Timestamp(Q)$

Now the transaction T_i has started before the latest write operation on data item (Q) has taken place. The T_i started to write on the data item (Q) but another transaction has written on it in between before T_i got a chance to write it. So it is now obsolete and again you have to reject and rollback.

Pictorially it can be shown as follows:

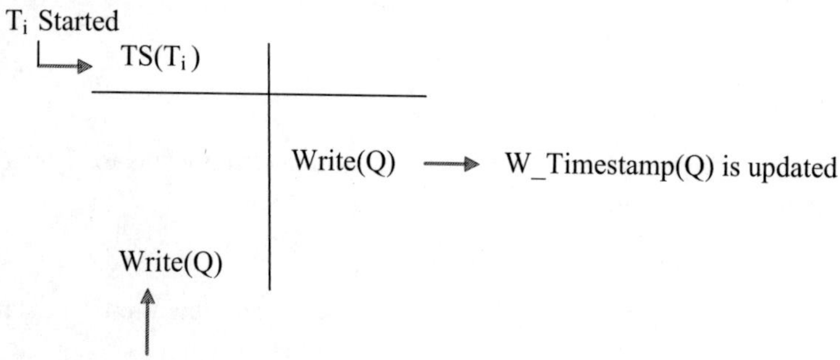

Here it has got a chance to write now, So writing on an already written value, therefore reject and rollback.

8.9 Validation Based Protocol

Validation based protocol takes a different view in solving the concurrency problem, and that is in reducing the concurrency overhead.

In lock based schemes, locks and unlocks are used which may create deadlocks.

In timestamp based scheme, since there are no locks involved, deadlock cannot occur, however the timestamps are compared. The timestamps of the transactions and read and write timestamps are compared during execution of the transaction. Each time an operation has to be performed, so this involves a lot of overhead and reduces the execution time of the concurrency control based schemes.

In validation based protocol, three phases are involved and no checking is done when the transaction is executing.

(1) Read Phase
(2) Validation Phase
(3) Write Phase

If the transaction has a read only operation, it will go through the read phase and validation phase. If the transaction has a write operation, it will go through the read phase, the validation phase and the write phase.

(1) Read Phase : In this phase, when a transaction T_i is executed. The values of various data items are read and stored in local variables of T_i. The write operation is performed only on the local variables of T_i without making any changes to the database.
(2) Validation Phase: In this phase the transaction T_i performs a test validating that it is ok to write the values of the variables to the actual database without compromising on the conflict serializability. When the test is passed the write phase is executed.
(3) Write Phase: If the validation phase is passed for the transaction $T_{i,}$ the system copies the updated values of local variables to the actual databases and updates the database, otherwise the transaction T_i is rolled back.

The three phases of the concurrently executing transactions can be interleaved.

To identify the various phases, the following timestamps are used:

(1) Start($T_{i)}$ - The time when the transaction T_i begins its execution.
(2) Validation (T_i) – The time when the transaction T_i finished its read phase and started its validation phase.
(3) Finish($T_{i)}$ – The time when T_i finished its write phase.

In the validation based protocol, the start of the transaction TS(T_i) = Validation(T_i), ie the transaction is assumed to be started when the validation phase begins and not at the start of the read phase.

If we have the following condition that

$$TS\ (T_{j)} < TS(T_k)$$

Then we say that in a serial schedule the transaction T_j has started before transaction T_k.

To choose validation(T_i) instead of start(T_i) as the start of the transaction T_i is to have better response time provided that the number of conflicts between transactions are less.

The Validation test for transaction T_j is as follows:

The test requires that one of the following conditions must be true for transaction T_j if TS(T_i) < TS(T_j) and for all transactions T_i.

(1) Finish (T_i) < Start (T_j)

This requires that T_i transaction has finished before the transaction T_j has started.

(T_i)	(T_j)
Finish(T_i)	
	Start (T_j)

Since there is no conflict, therefore conflict serializability is maintained.

2) The data items between T_i and T_j are not common, they work on different data items. What T_i writes on are different from what T_j reads on. Also T_i completes its write phase before T_j starts its validation phase.

i.e. Start (T_j) < Finish (T_i) < Validation (T_j)

(T_i)	(T_j)
	Start (T_j)
Finish(T_i)	
	Validation (T_j)

The writes of T_i and T_j do not overlap. The write of T_i do not affect the read of T_j. Also T_j does not affect the read of T_i. Therefore the serializability order is indeed maintained.

As an example illustration consider the following schedule:

(T_1)	(T_2)
Read(P)	
	Read(P)
	Read(Q)
Read(Q)	
<Validate>	
Display(P+Q)	
	<Validate>
	Write(P)
	Write(Q)

In transaction $T_{2,}$ write to the database is after the validation of T_2 and T_1 has read old values of P and Q. So it is serializable.

8.10 Granularity of Data Items

Granularity of data items the size of the data item under consideration. The data item can be of different sizes for example:

(a) A database record

(b) The field of a database record

(c) The file containing database record

(d) A disk block containing files

(e) The whole database

The above listed are the different granularities each of which is eligible to become a data item.

Small data items are called fine granularities and big data items are called coarse granularities. In whether it is advantageous to lock data items at finer granularity or at coarse granularity is to be seen.

For example, if in transaction T1 we lock a disk block B1 (coarse granularity), then all the files in that disk block will also get locked. Now if another transaction T2 wants to access a file in that disk block (B1), then it has to wait until the disk block B1 is unlocked.

On the other hand if we do fine grain granularity and a transaction T1 locks a record R1 of file F1, now if transaction T2 needs another record R2 from the same file F1, then it will need to lock R2 individually. This could have been prevented if I had locked the file F1 and the overhead of locking and unlocking of records individually could have been prevented.

So it is for the user to decide the appropriate size of the granularity of a data item chosen for locking.

8.10.1 Multiple Granularity Level Locking

The granularity level of locking is best decided by the transaction. The database which supports multiple levels of granularity work the best. In two phase locking, the lock can be requested at any level.

Let us consider an example, where shared and exclusive locks are used. Shared locks for reading of files, records, DB etc and exclusive for reading AND/OR writing o files records, blocks DB etc.

Now suppose that there is a file F1 which has a number of records R1, R2, ….Rn. If a transaction T1 wants to write to all records of file F1. If F1 is locked in exclusive mode, then all records of the file F1 ie R1, R2…Rn will be locked in exclusive mode and the transaction T1 would be able to write to all the records of F1.

Now suppose a transaction T2 comes which wants to read the record R2, now file F1 is locked in exclusive mode, so by compatibility matrix exclusive and shared cannot occur together, so T2 will be denied and it will not be able to read record R2.

Now suppose it happens the other way round. T2 comes before T1. So T2 wants to read record R2, so it locks R2 in shared mode. Now

T1 comes and wants to update all records R1, R2 ...Rn. So it has to lock F1 in exclusive mode, but now it is not possible to check each record separately whether it was locked in which mode to avoid conflicts. So here is where we introduce intension locks.

It is difficult for the lock manager to check all nodes which are children of current node for a lock conflict. This will become very inefficient and will cause delays.

Suppose there is another case in which transaction T1 wants to lock the entire database, so in that case it needs to lock the root of the database, but suppose a transaction T2 is holding a lock on a different granule in the tree say a file F1. So transaction T1 should not be able to proceed because part of the tree is locked, that part of the tree should be first unlocked only then the root could be locked. So the question is how does the root come to know whether any part of the tree is locked or not. In that case it needs to traverse the entire tree to find out, but that will take a lot of time and reduce the purpose of concurrency.

So to make multiple granularity easy to use, extra locks called intension locks are used.

The intension locks indicate that from the current node to the desired node, all along the path what type of lock can be requested on one of the children nodes of the current node.

For example,

(1) Intension-Shared (IS) says that a shared lock can be requested on some child node.

(2) Intension-Exclusive(IX) says that an exclusive lock can be requested on some child node.

(3) Shared-Intension-Exclusive(SIX) says that the current node is locked in shared mode but an exclusive lock can be requested on some child node.

The lock compatibility matrix is shown below for any two transactions Ti and Tj:

		Ti				
		IS	**IX**	**S**	**SIX**	**X**
Tj	**IS**	True	True	True	True	False
	IX	True	True	False	False	False
	S	True	False	True	False	False
	SIX	True	False	False	False	False
	X	False	False	False	False	False

The protocol that needs to be followed is known as multiple granularity locking protocol and is stated as follows:

1. The lock compatibility matrix should be followed.
2. The root of the the tree should be locked in any mode before locking any other node.
3. A child node can be locked in S or IS mode by a transaction, only if its parent node has been locked by the same transaction is IS or IX mode before.
4. A child node can be locked in X, IX and SIX mode by a transaction, only if its parent node has been locked by the same transaction in IX or SIX mode before.
5. A transaction can lock any node only if it has not unlocked any node. That is the two phase locking protocol is adhered to.
6. A transaction can unlock a node only if all its children are unlocked that is none of its child node is holding ant type of lock on itself.

To understand the protocol we must take an example,

(1) Suppose a transaction T1 wants to lock the database in shared mode.

(2) Suppose a transaction T2 wants to write to the record R13.

(3) Suppose a transaction T3 wants to read a record R16.

(4) Suppose a transaction t4 wants to read a fie F1.

The tree structure is shown as follows:

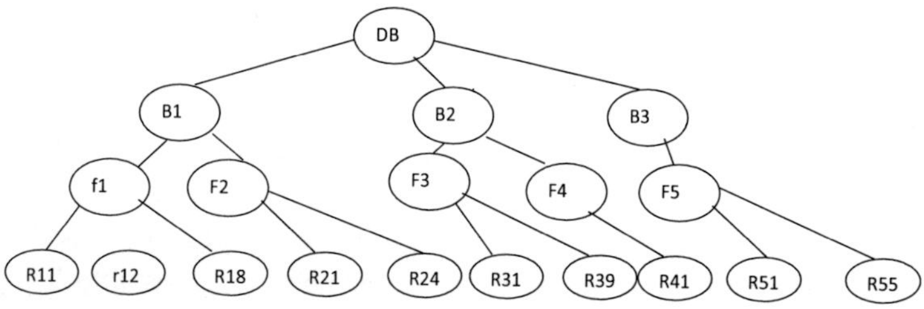

T1	t2	t3	t4
IS(DB)			
	IX(DB)		
	IX(B1)		
		IS(DB)	
		IS(B1)	
			IS(DB)
			IS(B1)
			S(F1)
		IS(F1)	
		S(r16)	
			Unlock(F1)
			Unlock(B1)
			Unlock(DB)
	IX(F1)		
	X(R13)		
	Unlock(R13)		
	Unlock(F1)		
	Unlock(B1)		
	Unlock(DB)		
		Unlock(R16)	
		Unlock(F1)	
		Unlock(B1)	
		Unlock(DB)	
Unlock(DB)			

Now T4 wants to read F1 and T2 wants to write R13. So T4 is holding a shared lock on F1 and T2 should lock F1 in IX mode so that it can lock R13 in X mode. Since a shared lock on F1 and an IX lock on F1 cannot coexist at the same time according to compatibility matrix, that is why we Unlock F1 in T4 which was locked in shared mode before locking F1 in Ix mode in T2. Since IX can exist with IS according to compatibility matrix so we have locked B1 in T2 in IX mode and B1 in T3 in IS mode one after another without unlocking B1 in T2. Also observe that two phase locking protocol is followed, once unlocking starts in any transaction, that transaction does not provide locks any further. Also observe first the children of any node are unlocked first before unlocking the parent node. So DB is unlocked at the end of every transaction.

8.11 Multiversion Schemes

The concept of timestamps is used in Multiverion Schemes.

Every Transaction Ti in the system has a unique static timestamp given to it TS(Ti) which denotes the beginning of the transaction Ti. This timetstamp is assigned to te transaction before the transaction stars its execution.

Every data item Qk has a sequence of versions which can be given to it in the form of < Q1, Q2, ….Qn> . Each version Qk has been associated with 3 fields:

(1) The content of Qk or the value given to Qk.
(2) The W-Timestamp (Qk) is the timestamp of the transaction (i.e. TS(Ti)) whci had created the version Qk.
(3) R_Timestamp (Qk) is the largest Timestamp of any transaction that had read the version Qk successfully.

A new version of atransaction say Ti is created whenever the data item Q has issueed a Write(Q) operation.

The content field then of the new version contains the value which has just been written by the transaction Ti.

Thw W-Timestamp and R_Timestamp of TS(Ti) get re-initialized here.

If another transaction Tj reads the value of the version Qk sometime later on such that

R_Timetamp(Qk) < TS (Tj)

Then the R_timestamp (Qk) gets updated.

The Multiversion Timestamp Ordering Scheme:

It has the following Properties:

(1) It ensures serializability

(2) If a transaction Ti issues a Read(Q) or Write(Q) operation then,

Let Qk be denoted as the verion of Q for which the W_Timestamp (Qk) is the larges and also

W_Timestamp(Qk) < = TS(Ti)

Then the sequence of evens are shown as follows:

W_Timestamp(Qk)

TS(Ti)

R_Timestamp(Qk)

Read(Q)

Write(Q)

(1) If the transaction Ti issues a Read(Q) then it is safe, The operation Read(Q) is done before Write(Q) so the value returned to the Read(Q) is the contents of the versin of Qk.

(2) If the transction Ti issues a Write(Q) and aslo TS(Ti) < R_ Timestamp(Qk), then the system Rolls Bac, because TS(Ti) had started to do a Write operation and some other transction has done a Read(Q) before I could get a chance to do Write(Q), so the transaction whichnhas done Read(Q) gets an older value and not the updated value which would have been given by performing the Write(Q) opeartion .

On the other hand if

TS(Ti) = W_Timestamp(Qk)

And a Write(Q) operation is issued.

TS(Ti) W_timestamp(Qk)

Write(Q)

The system overwrites the contents of Qk oe else it creates a new version of Qk.

To Summarize, the 2 rules just explained above are as follows:

(1) The first rule states that it reads the most recent version Qk if the Read(Q) statement comes on time.

(2) The Second rule aborts the transaction and rolls back if it was too late for doing a Write(Q).

Or it can be stated as if Ti tries to write version of Q that some other transaction has already read, then we cannot allow that write to take place.

Otherwise a new version of Qk is created.

SOLUTIONS TO IMPORTANT QUESTIONS IN DBMS

Q1. Construct an ER diagram for a hospital with a set of patients and a set of medical doctors. Associate with each patient a log of the various tests and examinations conducted. Map your ER diagram to the relational model.

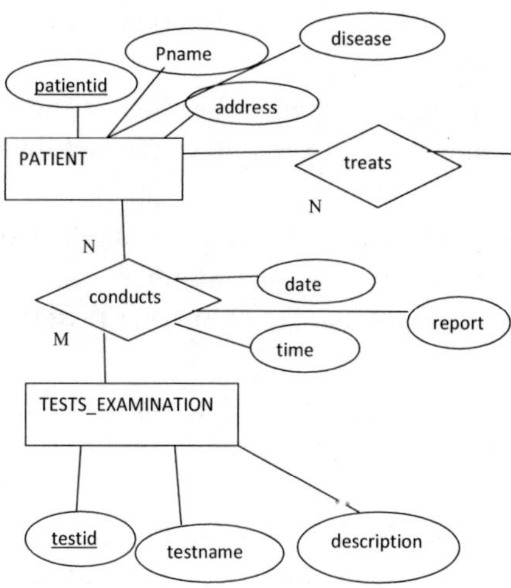

The relational Model will be as follows :

PATIENT

patientid	pname	address	disease	docid

PK FK

DOCTORS

Docid	docname	specialization

PK

TESTS_EXAMINATIONS

Testid	testname	description

PK

CONDUCTS

patientid	Testid	date	time	report

← PK →

(Q2) Suppose we informally define the data in the database of a department store as follows:

(1) Each employee is represented. The data about an employee are his employee number, name, address and the department he works for.

(2) Each department is represented. The data about a department are its name, employees, manager and items sold.

(3) Each items sold is represented. The data about an item are its name, manufacturer, price, model number (assigned by manufacturer) and an internal item number (assigned by the store).

(4) Each manufacturer is represented. The data about a manufacturer are its name, address, items supplied to the store and their prices.

Give an entity relationship diagram for this database. Note that some information may be represented by attributes, other information may be represented by relationship.

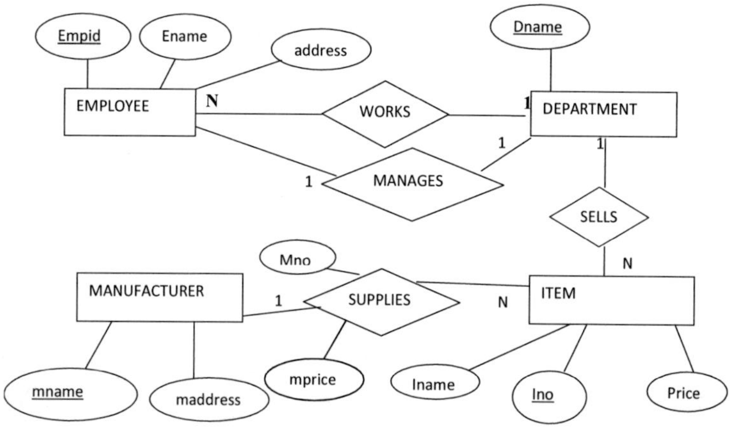

(Q3) A Company database needs to store information about employees (identified by SSN, with salary and phone as attribute), departments (identified by dno, with dname, and budget as attributes) and children of employees (with name and age as attributes). Employees work in departments; each department is managed by an employee; a child must be identified uniquely by name when the parent(who is an employee ; assume that only one parent works for the company) is known. We are not interested in information about a child once the parent leaves the company.

Draw an ER diagram that captures this information using the concepts and notations of ER.

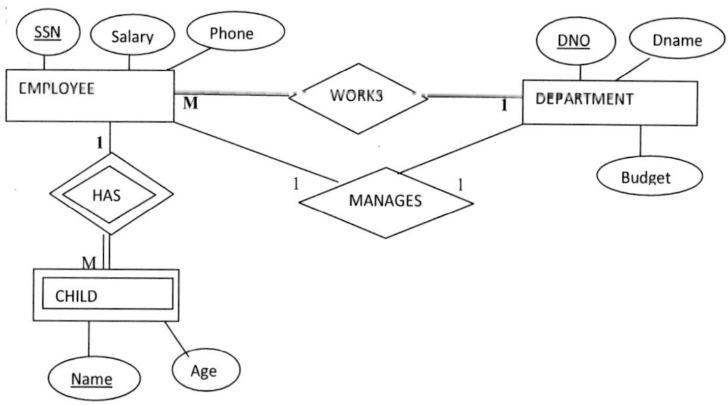

(Q4) Construct an ER Diagram for your institute with a set of teachers and set of students. Teachers offer various subjects to different classes.

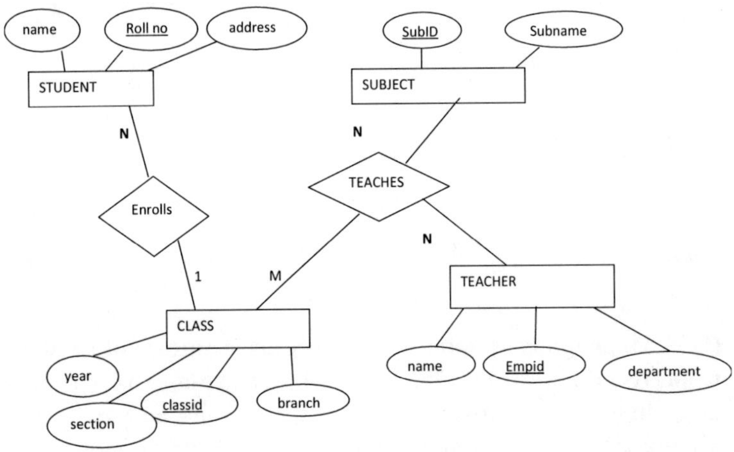

(Q5) Create an ER diagram for university registrar office. The office maintains data about each class, each instructor teaching in the class, no of students enrolled, no of subjects for each class, and the time and date of class held. For each student-subject pair a grade is also recorded. Take suitable assumptions if required.

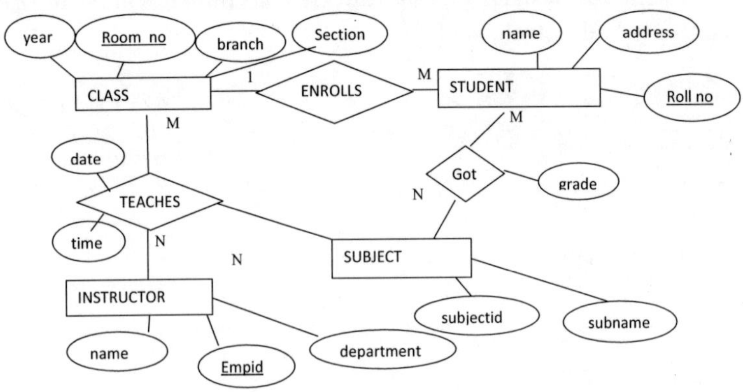

RELATIONAL ALGEBRA

(1) Consider the following relation schema:

SUPPLIER(sid: integer, sname: string, address: string)

PARTS(pid: integer,pname: string, color: string)

CATALOG(sid: integer,pid: integer, cost: real)

The Catalog relation lists the prices charged for parts by Suppliers: Express the following statements into relational algebra expressions.

(1) Find the supplier names of the suppliers who supply a red part that costs less than 100 dollars.

$$PART\_CAT <- (PARTS \bowtie_{PID = PID} CATALOG)$$

$$A< - \Pi_{Sid}(\sigma_{Cost<100 \wedge Color=\text{'Red'}} (PART\_CAT))$$

$$RESULT <- \Pi_{Sname}(A \bowtie_{SID = SID} SUPPLIER)$$

(2) Find the supplier names of the suppliers who supply a red part that costs less than 100 dollars and a green part that costs less than 100 dollars.

$$PART\_CAT <- (PARTS \bowtie_{PID = PID} CATALOG)$$

$$A< - \Pi_{Sid}(\sigma_{Cost<100 \wedge Color=\text{'Green'}} (PART\_CAT))$$

$$B < - \Pi_{Sid}(\Pi_{Cost<100 \wedge Color=\text{'Red'}} (PART\_CAT))$$

$$C< - A \cap B$$

$$RESULT \quad <- \Pi_{Sname}(C \bowtie_{SID = SID} SUPPLIER)$$

(3) Find the supplier ids of the suppliers who supply a red part that costs less than 100 dollars and a green part that costs less than 100 dollars.

$$PART\_CAT <- (PARTS \bowtie_{PID = PID} CATALOG)$$

$A <- \Pi_{Sid}(\sigma_{Cost<100 \wedge Color='Green'} (PART\_CAT))$

$B <- \Pi_{Sid}(\sigma_{Cost<100 \wedge Color='Red'} (PART\_CAT))$

$RESULT <- \Pi_{Sid} (A \cap B)$

(2) Consider the following relation schema:

STUDENT(RollNo, Name, Father_Name, Branch)

BOOK(ISBN, Title, Author, Publisher)

ISSUE(RollNo, ISBN, Date-of_issue)

Write the following queries in Relational Algebra:

(a) List Roll Number and Name of all students of the branch CSE.

$\Pi_{RollNo, Name}(\sigma_{branch='CSE'} (STUDENT))$

(b) Find the name of students who have issued a book published by 'ABC' publisher.

$ISBN\_ABC <- \Pi_{ISBN}(\sigma_{publisher='ABC'} (BOOK))$

$ABC\_STUDENT <- \Pi_{RollNo}(ISSUE \bowtie_{ISBN = ISBN} ISBN\_ABC)$

$RESULT <- \Pi_{Name} (STUDENT \bowtie_{RollNo = Roll No} ABC\_STUDENT)$

(c) List title of all books and their author issued by a student 'XYZ'

$ROLLNO\_XYZ <- \Pi_{RollNo} (\sigma_{Name='XYZ'} (STUDENT))$

$ISBN\_XYZ <- \Pi_{ISBN} (ISSUE \bowtie_{ROLLNO = ROLLNO} ROLLNO\_XYZ)$

$RESULT <- \Pi_{Title, Author} (BOOK \bowtie_{ISBN = ISBN} ISBN\_XYZ)$

(d) List title of all books issued on or before Jan 1, 2011.

$ISBN\_BEFORE\_JAN <- \Pi_{ISBN} (\sigma_{Date-of-Issue<'01/01/2011'} (ISSUE))$

$RESULT <- \Pi_{Title} (BOOK \bowtie_{ISBN = ISBN} ISBN\_BEFORE\_JAN)$

(e) List all books published by publisher 'ABC'

$\Pi_{ISBN,\ Title,\ Author}(\sigma_{publisher='ABC'}$ (BOOK))

(3) Consider the following relation schema:

VEHICLE(reg_no, make, color)

PERSON(eno, name, address)

OWNER(eno, reg_no)

Write expressions in relational algebra to answer the following queries:

(1) List the names of persons who do not own any car

ALL_PERSONS <- Π_{eno} (PERSON)

PERSON_WITH_CARS <- Π_{eno} (PERSON $\bowtie_{ENO = ENO}$ OWNER)

RESULT <- Π_{eno} (ALL_PERSONS - PERSON_WITH_CARS)

(2) List the names of persons who own only maruti cars.

R (eno, no_of_cars) < - eno$\delta_{Count\ (reg_no)}$ (OWNER)

WITH_ONE_CAR <- Π_{eno} ($\sigma_{no\_of\_cars\ =\ 1}$ (R))

PEOPLE_WITH_ONE_CAR <- (OWNER $\bowtie_{ENO = ENO}$ WITH_ONE_CAR)

PEOPLE_WITH_MARUTI_CAR <- Π_{reg_no} ($\sigma_{make\ =\ 'maruti'}$ (VEHICLE))

ENO_MARUTI <- Π_{eno} (PEOPLE_WITH_MARUTI_CAR $\bowtie_{Reg\_no = Reg\_no}$ PEOPLE_WITH_ONE_CAR)

RESULT <- Π_{name} (PERSONS $\bowtie_{eno = eno}$ ENO_MARUTI)

(3) List the names of persons who own 3 or more than 3 cars.

R (eno, no_of_cars) < - eno$\delta_{Count\ (reg_no)}$ (OWNER)

R2 <- Π_{eno} ($\sigma_{no\_of\_cars>=3}$ (R))

RESULT <- Π_{name} (PERSONS $\bowtie_{eno = eno}$ R2)

(4) Consider the following relation schema:

STUDENT(ssn, name, address, major)

COURSE(code, title)

REGISTERED (ssn, code)

Write expressions in relational algebra to answer the following queries:

(1) List the codes of courses in which at least one student is registered (registered courses)

RESULT <- Π_{code} (REGISTERED)

(2) List the title of registered courses.

R1<- (COURSE REGISTERED)

CODE =CODE

RESULT <- Π_{title} (R1)

(3) List the codes of courses for which no student is registered.

ALL_COURSES <- Π_{code} (COURSE)

REG_COURSES <- Π_{code} (REGISTERED)

NO_REG_COURSES <- Π_{code} (ALL_COURSES - REG_COURSES)

(4) The title of courses for which no student is registered.

ALL_COURSES<- Π_{code} (COURSE)

REG_COURSES <- Π_{code} (REGISTERED)

NO_REG_COURSES <- Π_{code} (ALL_COURSES - REG_COURSES)

RESULT <- Π_{title} (NO_REG_COURSES $\bowtie_{CODE = CODE}$ COURSE)

(5) Names of students and the title of courses they are registered to.

REG_STUDENT < - (REGISTERED $\bowtie_{SSN = SSN}$ STUDENT)

$$REG\_COURSE\_STUD <- (REG\_STUDENT \bowtie_{CODE=CODE} COURSE)$$

$$RESULT <- \Pi_{name,\ title} (REG\_COURSE\_STUD)$$

(6) SSN of student who are registered for both 'DataBase Systems' and 'Analysis of Algorithms'

$$DBMS <- \sigma_{title = \text{'DataBase Systems'}} (COURSE)$$

$$ALGO <- \sigma_{title = \text{'Analysis of Algorithms'}} (COURSE)$$

$$A <- \Pi_{ssn} (DBMS \bowtie_{CODE=CODE} REGISTERED)$$

$$B <- \Pi_{ssn} (ALGO \bowtie_{CODE=CODE} REGISTERED)$$

$$RESULT <- \Pi_{ssn} (A \cap B)$$

(7) The name of students who are registered for both 'DataBase Systems' and 'Analysis of Algorithms'

$$DBMS <- \sigma_{title = \text{'DataBase Systems'}} (COURSE)$$

$$ALGO <- \sigma_{title = \text{'Analysis of Algorithms'}} (COURSE)$$

$$A <- \Pi_{ssn} (DBMS \bowtie_{CODE=CODE} REGISTERED)$$

$$B <- \Pi_{ssn} (ALGO \bowtie_{CODE=CODE} REGISTERED)$$

$$C <- \Pi_{ssn} (A \cap B)$$

$$RESULT <- \Pi_{name} (C \bowtie_{SSN=SSN} STUDENT)$$

(8) List of courses in which all students are registered.

$$ALL\_STUDENT <- \Pi_{ssn} (STUDENT)$$

$$REG\_STUDENT <- \Pi_{ssn,\ code} (REGISTERED)$$

$$COURSE\_STUD <- \Pi_{code} (REG\_STUDENT \div ALL\_STUDENT)$$

$$RESULT <- \Pi_{title} (COURSE\_STUD \bowtie_{CODE=CODE} COURSE)$$

(9) List of courses in which all 'ECMP' major students are registered

ECMP_STUD <- Π_{ssn} ($\sigma_{major = 'ECMP'}$ (STUDENT))

REG_STUDENT <- $\Pi_{ssn, code}$ (REGISTERED)

COURSE_STUD <- Π_{code} (REG_STUDENT ÷ ECMP_STUD)

RESULT<- Π_{title} (COURSE_STUD $\bowtie_{CODE=CODE}$ COURSE)

(5) Consider the following relation schema:

FLIGHTS(flno, from, to, distance, departs)

AIRCRAFT(aid, aname, range)

CERTIFIED(eid, aid)

EMPLOYEES(eid, ename,salary)

By definition, pilots are those employees who are certified on at least one aircraft. An aircraft can be used for any flight provided it has sufficient range. Pilots can pilot any flight provided they are certified on an aircraft with sufficient range. Write expressions in relational algebra to answer the following queries:

1. Find eid's of pilots who are certified on some Boeing.

   R1 <- $\sigma_{aname = 'Boeing'}$ (AIRCRAFT)

   R2<- R1 $\bowtie_{AID = AID}$ CERTIFIED

   RESULT < -Π_{eid} (R2)

2. Find names of pilots who are certified on some Boeing.

   R1 <- $\sigma_{aname = 'Boeing'}$ (AIRCRAFT)

   R2<- R1 $\bowtie_{AID = AID}$ CERTIFIED

   R3<- R2 $\bowtie_{EID=EID}$ EMPLOYEES

   RESULT < -Π_{ename} (R3)

3. Find aid's of aircraft that can fly non-stop from 'LA' to 'NY'. Assume you don't already know the distance.

   R1 <- $\sigma_{\text{from = 'LA' AND to = 'NY'}}$ (FLIGHTS)

   R2<- R1 $\bowtie_{\text{DISTANCE <= RANGE}}$ AIRCRAFT

   RESULT < -Π_{aid} (R2)

4. Find flno of flights that can be piloted by every pilot whose salary is over Rs. 100,000.

   R1 <- $\sigma_{\text{salary > 100000}}$ (EMPLOYEES)

   R2 (AID) <- Π_{aid} (R1 $\bowtie_{\text{EID=EID}}$ CERTIFIED)

   R3 (FLNO, AID) <- $\Pi_{\text{FLNO, AID}}$ (FLIGHTS $\bowtie_{\text{DISTANCE <= RANGE}}$ AIRCRAFT)

   RESULT < -Π_{FLNO} (R3 $\div$ R2)

SQL QUERIES

(Q1) Consider the following Relation Schema:

EMP(eid: integer, ename: string, age: integer, salary: real)

WORKS(eid: integer, did: integer,pcttime: integer)

DEPT (did: integer, dname: string,budget: real, managerid: integer)

Answer each of the following questions briefly in SQL:

(1) Give an example of a foreign key constraint that involves the DEPT relation. What are the options for enforcing this constraint when a user attempts to delete a DEPT tuple?

The did field of WORKS should be a foreign key that refers to DEPT relation.

```
CREATE TABLE WORKS      (eid integer not null,
                         did integer not null,
                         pcttime integer,
                         PRIMARY KEY (eid, did)
                         FOREIGN KEY (did) REFERENCES
                            DEPT (did));
```

The different options for maintaining referential integrity when the user attempts to delete a DEPT tuple are:

(1) ON DELETE CASCADE- Setting this option results in deletion of those tuples from WORKS relation that refer to the value of did of the tuple being deleted from DEPT relation.

(2) ON DELETE SET DEFAULT – Setting this option results in setting a default value to did in those of WORKS relation that refer to the value of did of the tuple being deleted from DEPT relation.

(3) ON DELETE SET NULL - Setting this option results in setting a NULL value to did in those of WORKS relation that refer to the value of did of the tuple being deleted from DEPT relation.

(2) Write SQL statements required to create the preceding relations, including appropriate versions of all primary and foreign key integrity constraints

```
CREATE TABLE EMP        (eid integer not null,
                         ename varchar2(20),
                         age integer,
                         salary REAL,
                         PRIMARY KEY (eid));

CREATE TABLE WORKS      (eid integer not null,
                         did integer not null,
                         pcttime integer,
                         PRIMARY KEY (eid, did),
                         FOREIGN KEY (did) REFERENCES DEPT (did),
                         FOREIGN KEY (eid) REFERENCES EMP (eid),
                         ON DELETE CASCADE);

CREATE TABLE DEPT       (did integer not null,
                         dname varchar2(20),
                         budget REAL,
                         managerid integer,
                         PRIMARY KEY (did),
                         FOREIGN KEY (managerid) REFERENCES
                            EMP (eid),
                         ON DELETE SET NULL);
```

(3) Define the DEPT relation in SQL so that every department is guaranteed to have manager.

```
CREATE TABLE DEPT       (did integer not null,
                         dname varchar2(20),
                         budget REAL,
                         managerid integer not null,
                         PRIMARY KEY (did),
                         FOREIGN KEY (managerid)
                         REFERENCES EMP (eid));
```

(4) Write an SQL statement to add John Doe as an employee with eid = 101, age = 32 and salary = 15,000.

```
INSERT INTO EMP VALUES (101, 'John Doe',32, 15000);
```

(5) Write an SQL statement to give every employee a 10 percent raise.

```
UPDATE EMP
SET salary = salary * 1.10;
```

(Q2) Consider the following schema for student database of an institute:

TEACHER(TeacherID, Tname, Department)

STUDENT(RollNo, Sname, Branch)

TEACHES(TeacherID, Roll No, Subject)

Write the following queries:

(1) Write SQL statements to create the above database.

CREATE TABLETEACHER(TeacherID varchar2(20), Tname varchar2(30), Department varchar2(20));

CREATE TABLE STUDENT(RollNo varchar2(10), Sname varchar2(30), Branch varchar2(20));

CREATE TABLETEACHES(TeacherID varchar2(20), RollNo varchar2(10), Subject varchar2(20));

(2) Write SQL statements to insert one record to each table. The data can suitably be assumed.

INSERT INTO TEACHERVALUES ('T101', 'Gunjan Gupta', 'IT');

INSERT INTO STUDENTVALUES ('S1011', 'Amitkumar', 'CS');

INSERT INTO TEACHESVALUES ('T101, 'S1011', 'DBMS',);

(3) List the name and branch of student registered for the subject 'DBMS'.

SELECTSname, Branch

FROM STUDENT, TEACHES

WHERE STUDENT.RollNo = TEACHES.RollNo

AND subject = 'DBMS';

(4) List the name of the teachers and their corresponding department who are offering either 'DBMS' or 'Operating System'.

SELECT Distinct Tname, Department

FROM TEACHER

WHERE TeacherID IN (SELECTTeacherId

FROM TEACHES

```
WHERE Subject = 'DBMS')
OR TeacherID IN (SELECTTeacherId
                 FROM TEACHES
                 WHERE Subject = 'Operating System');
```

(5) List the name of students who are being taught by teachers of CSE Department.

```
SELECT Sname
FROM STUDENT, TEACHES,TEACHER
WHERE STUDENT.RollNo = TEACHES.RollNo
AND TEACHER.TeacherID = TEACHES.TeacherId
AND Department = 'CSE';
```

(Q3) specify the following queries in SQL based on the given schema:

supplier(sid, sname, city)

part(pid, pname, color)

SP(sid, pid, quantity)

(1) Get the names of suppliers whose name begins with R

```
SELECT sname
FROM supplier
WHERE sname like 'R%';
```

(2) Get pairs of supplier numbers that both operate from same city

```
SELECT a.sid ,b.sid
FROM supplier as A, supplier as B
WHERE A.city = B.city;
```

(3) Get the names of suppliers who supply part P2

```
SELECTsname
FROM supplier, SP
WHERE supplier.sid = SP.sid
AND pid = 'P2';
```

(4) Get the supplier id and the names of suppliers in descending order of city.

```
SELECT sid, sname
```

```
FROM supplier
ORDER BY city desc;
```

(Q4) For the following relational schema

STUDENT (Name, Roll_No, Address, Course)

ADMISSION (Roll_No,Course, Semester)

FACULTY (Course, Faculty_Name, Semester)

OFFERING (Branch, Course)

Give an expression in SQL for each of the following queries:

(1) Students who have taken all courses offered by the faculty 'Raghunandan'

```
SELECT Name
FROM STUDENT AS S1
WHERE (SELECT Course
                FROM STUDENT AS S2
                WHERE S1.Roll_No = S2.Roll_no
                CONTAINS
                SELECT COURSE
                FROM FACULTY
                WHERE Faculty_Name = 'Raghunandan')
```

(2) All the courses taken by student 'Amit'

```
SELECT    Course
FROM      STUDENT
WHERE     Name = 'Amit'
```

(3) Name all the faculty who had taught student 'Amit'

```
SELECT    Faculty_Name
FROM      FACULTY, STUDENT, ADMISSION
WHERE     Name = 'Amit'
AND       FACULTY.Course = ADMISSION.  Course
AND       FACULTY.Semester = ADMISSION.Semester
AND       AMISSION.Roll_No= STUDENT.Roll_No
```

(4) Find the names of all students who are studying in 'Audit' Courses.

```
SELECT    Name
```

```
FROM     STUDENT
WHERE    Course = 'Audit'
```

(Q5) For the following relational schema

EMPLOYEE(EID, EmployeeName, Street, City, Deptt, CompanyName)

COMPANY(CompanyName, City)

WORKS(EmployeeName, CompanyName, Salary)

MANAGES(EmployeeName, ManagerName)

Give an expression in SQL for each of the following queries:

(1) Find out the names of all employees that have 'A' anywhere in their Name and are in department 'IT'

```
SELECT EmployeeName
FROM EMPLOYEE
WHERE Deptt = 'IT'
AND EmployeeName like '%A%'
```

(2) List the names of Departments in ascending Order and their employee in descending order.

```
SELECT    Deptt, EmployeeName
FROM      EMPLOYEE
ORDER BY  Deptt, EmployeeName DESC
```

(3) Find the Names, City, Deptt of all employees who work in 'TCS'

```
SELECT    EmployeeName, City, Deptt
FROM      EMPLOYEE
WHERE     CompanyName = 'TCS'
```

(4) Find the names of employees whose salary is more than 30000.

```
SELECT    EmployeeName
FROM      WORKS
WHERE     Salary > 30000
```

(5) List all Manager Names.

```
SELECT    DISTINCT ManagerName
FROM      MANAGES
```

(Q6) For the following relational schema

PERSON(Driver_id, Name, Address)

CAR(License, Model, Year)

ACCIDENT(Report_No, Date, Location)

OWNS(Driver_id, License)

PARTICIPATED(Driver_id, License, Report_No, Damage_ Amount)

Give an expression in SQL for each of the following queries:

(1) Find the total number of persons who owned cars that met with Accidents in 2010.

```
SELECT    count(*)
FROM      ACCIDENT, PARTICIPATED, OWNS
WHERE     Date like '%2010%'
AND       ACCIDENT.Report_No = PARTICIPATED.Report_no
AND       OWNS.Driver_id = PARTICIPATED.Driver_id
AND       OWNS.License = PARTICIPATED.License
```

2) Find the total number of accidents in which the cars belonging to 'Abhay' were involved

```
SELECT    Count(*)
FROM      PERSON, PARTICIPATED, CAR, OWNS
WHERE     Name = 'Abhay'
AND       PERSON.Driver_id = OWNS.Driver_id
AND       CAR.License = OWNS.License
AND       OWNS.Driver_id = PARTICIPATED.Driver_id
AND       OWNS.License = PARTICIPATED.License
AND       ACCIDENT.Report_no = PARTICIPATED.Report_No.
```

(3) Add a new acci9dent to the datbse with report_no = 'AR101', Current date and location 'Noida'

```
Insert into ACCIDENT values ('AR101', '26-Sep-2018', 'Noida')
```

(4) Find the Damage Amount for the Driver_id = 'D001'

```
SELECT    SUM(Damage_Amount)
FROM      PARTICIPATED
WHERE     Driver_id = 'D001'
```

(Q5) For the following relational schema:

STUDENT(Roll_No, Name, Branch, Year, Section, Hostel, Father_Name, Address)

BOOK(Book_Id, Title, Author, Publisher,Cost,Copies)

TRANSACTION(Roll_No, Book_Id, Date_Issue, Date_Return, Fine)

Give an expression in SQL for each of the following queries:

(1) To add a new field DOB in the Student table.

```
ALTER TABLE STUDENT ADD DOB DATE
```

(2) To drop a column fine from the Transaction Table.

```
ALTER TABLE TRANSACTION DROP COLUMN FINE
```

(3) Delete all entries from the Hostel column of student table.

```
UPDATE STUDENT
SET Hostel = “”
```

(4) To display all books which have been issued so far.

```
SELECT DISTINCT Book_id, Title, Author
FROM BOOK, TRANSACTION
WHERE BOOK.Book_id = TRANSACTION.Book_id
```

(5) To display all books which have not been issued so far.

```
SELECT DISTINCT Book_id, Title, Author
FROM BOOK
WHERE Book_id NOT IN (SELECT DISTINCT Book_id
                      FROM TRANSACTION )
```

(6) To display names of students who have not returned the books issued to them

```
SELECT Name
FROM STUDENT
WHERE Roll_No IN  (SELECT Roll_no
                   FROM TRANSACTION
                   WHERE Date_Return = NULL )
```

(7) To display names of students who have been issued 'DBMS' Book by 'KORTH'

```
SELECT Name
FROM STUDENT, BOOK, TRANSACTION
WHERE STUDENT. Roll_No= TRANSACTION.Roll_No
AND BOOK.Book_Id = TRANSACTION.Book_Id
AND Author = 'KORTH'
AND Title = 'DBMS'
```

(8) To display names of students who have not been issued any book so far.

```
SELECT Name
FROM STUDENT
WHERE Roll_NoNOT IN        (SELECT DISTINCT Roll_no
                            FROM TRANSACTION )
```

(9) To display names of students who have been issued at least one book.

```
SELECT Name
FROM STUDENT, TRANSACTION
WHERE STUDENT. Roll_No= TRANSACTION.Roll_No
```

(10) To display the title of second costliest book

```
SELECT Title, MAX(Cost)
FROM BOOK
WHERE Cost IN (SELECT Cost
               FROM BOOK
               MINUS
               SELECT MAX(Cost)
               FROM BOOK )
```

(11) To display the student names who have been issued 'DBMS' book by 'KORTH' and 'OS' book by 'TANNENBAUM'

```
SELECT    Name
FROM      STUDENT, BOOK, TRANSACTION
WHERE     STUDENT.Roll_No = TRANSACTION.Roll_No
AND       BOOK.Book_id = TRANSACTION.Book_id
```

```
AND       Title = 'DBMS'
AND       Author = 'KORTH'

INTERSECT

SELECT    Name
FROM      STUDEENT, BOOK, TRANSACTION
WHERE     STUDENT.Roll_No = TRANSACTION.Roll_No
AND       BOOK.Book_id = TRANSACTION.Book_id
AND       Title = 'OS'
AND       Author = 'TANNENBAUM'
```

(12) To display the student names who have been issued 'DBMS' book by 'KORTH' or 'OS' book by 'TANNENBAUM'

```
SELECT    Name
FROM      STUDENT, BOOK, TRANSACTION
WHERE     STUDENT.Roll_No = TRANSACTION.Roll_No
AND       BOOK.Book_id = TRANSACTION.Book_id
AND       Title = 'DBMS'
AND       Author = 'KORTH'

UNION

SELECT    Name
FROM      STUDEENT, BOOK, TRANSACTION
WHERE     STUDENT.Roll_No = TRANSACTION.Roll_No
AND       BOOK.Book_id = TRANSACTION.Book_id
AND       Title = 'OS'
AND       Author = 'TANNENBAUM'
```

(13) To display the student names who have NOT been issued 'DBMS' book by 'KORTH'

```
SELECT    Name
FROM      STUDENT
WHERE     Roll_NoIN (SELECT Roll_No
                   FROM STUDENT
                   MINUS
                   SELECT Roll_No
```

```
                FROM STUDENT, BOOK, TRANSACTION
                WHERE STUDENT.Roll_No = TRANSACTION.
                Roll_No
                AND BOOK.Book_id = TRANSACTION.Book_id
                AND Title = 'DBMS'
AND Author = 'KORTH')
```

(14) To Count the number of books issued by each student.

```
SELECT Roll_No, COUNT(*)
FROM STUDENT, TRANSACTION
WHERE STUDENT.Roll_No = TRANSACTION.Roll_No
GROUP BY (Roll_No)
```

(Q6) For the following relational schema:

EMPLOYEE(EmpId, EmpName, Street, City)

WORKS(EmpId, CompId, Salary)

COMPANY(CompId, CompName, City)

Give an expression in SQL for each of the following queries:

(1) Find the names of employees whose salary is more than the average salary of all employees of their company.

```
SELECT    empname
FROM      employee, works
WHERE     empid = empid
AND       salary > (SELECT avg(salary)
          FROM   works
          WHERE empid = empid
          GROUP BY compid)
```

(2) Find the names of companies that has the largest number of employees.

```
SELECT    compname, count(*)
FROM      company, works
WHERE     compid = compid
GROUP BY compid
HAVING count(*) > all (SELECT count(*)
                     FROM works
                     GROUP BY compid )
```

(3) Find names of employees whose salary is more than that of every employee of company named 'ABCD'.

```
SELECTempname
FROM employee, works
WHEREempid = empid
AND salary>( SELECT max (salary)
            FROM company, works
            WHEREcompname = 'ABCD'
            ANDcompid = compid )
```

(4) Find names of companies located in the city in which company 'ABCD' is located.

```
SELECTcompname
FROM company
WHERE city in (SELECT city
              FROM company
              WHEREcompname = 'ABCD')
```

(5) Give all employees a 20 percent raise in salary whose city is different from the city they work in.

```
UPDATE works
SET salary = salary * 1.20
WHEREempid in (SELECTempid
              FROM employee
              WHERE city not in (SELECT city
                         FROM works, company, employee
                         WHEREcompid = compid
                         AND empid = empid) )
```

JOIN DECOMPOSITIONS, CLOSURE and KEYS

(1) Suppose we have a database for an investment firm, consisting of the following attributes: B(broker), O(office of the broker), I(investor), S(stock), Q(quantity of stock owned by an investor) and D(dividend paid by a stock) with the functional dependencies:

S-> D

I -> B

IS -> Q

B ->O

(1) Find a key for the relation schema R = BOSQID

(2) How many key does relation schema R have? Justify

(3) Find a decomposition of R into third normal form having a lossless join and preserving dependencies.

Ans.

(1) $S^+ = D$

$I^+ = BO$

$(IS)^+ = BOQDIS$ contains all attributes therefore IS is a key.

(2) IS is the only key in R.

(3) S-> D

I -> B

IS -> Q

B -> O

$\{S\}^+ = S, D$

$\{I\}^+ = I, R, O$

$\{IS\}^+ = I, S, Q, B, D, O$

There fore IS is the key

In 3rd normal form make a table for every dependency and see that there are no trivial dependencies and no partial dependencies and see that a table contains the key.

R1 = I, S, Q

R2= S, D

R3 = I, B

R4 = B, O

There are no trivial and partial dependencies in this decomposition therefore it is in 3NF.

Also one relation R1 contains the key.

(Q2) Reduce the following relation into 2NF and 3NF decompositions with the following dependencies.

R = { A B C D E F G H I J }

A, B -> C

A-> D, E

B -> F

F -> G, H

D ->I, J

Ans)

$\{A\}^+$ = A, D, E, I, J

$\{B\}^+$ = B, F, G, H

Therefore AB is the Key.

For 2NF decomposition, the following relations do not have any partial dependency:

R1 = A, D, E, I, J where A is the Key

R2 = B, F, G, H where B is the Key

R3 = A, B, C since there was no relation containing the key AB

For 3NF there should not be any transitive dependency.

Now R1 has transitive dependency as A -> D, E

And D-> I, J

Therefore we need to decompose R1 into

R11 = A, D, E

R12 = D, I, J

R2 has transitive dependency as B-> F

And F -> G, H

Therefore we need to decompose R2 into

R22 = B, F

R23 = F, G, H

Therefore the number of relations for 3 NF decompositions are

R11 = A, D, E where A is the Key

R12 = D, I, J where D is the Key

R22 = B, F where B is the key

R23 = F, G, H where F is the key

R3 = A, B, C where AB is the key

(Q3) Reduce the following relation into 2NF and 3NF decompositions with the following dependencies.

R = { A B C D E F G H I J }

A, B -> C

B, D -> E, F

A, D, -> G, H

A -> I

H -> J

Ans)

$\{A,B\}^+$ -> C

$\{A,B\}^+$ -> C, A, B, I

$\{B, D\}^+$ -> B, D, E, F

$\{A, D\}^+$ -> A, D, G,H, I,J

There {A, B, D} is the key.

R1 = {A, B, D} since there is no elation that contains the key, so we form a relation alone that contains the key.

From the closures we form the following relations

R2 = {A, B, C, I} where AB is the key

R3 = {B, D, E, F } where B, D is the key

R4 = { A, D, G, H, J, I } where A,D is the key

Now R2 and R4 are not in 2NF because there is a partial dependency A -> I

Therefore we need to decompose R2 and R4 as

R2 = {A, B, C}

R4 = {A, D, G, H, J}

R5 = {A, I} where A is the key

So the final relations for 2NF are :

R1 = {A, B, D} where ABD is the key

R2 = {A, B, C} where AB is the Key

R3 = {B, D, E, F } where B, D is the key

R4 = {A, D, G, H, J} where AD is the key

R5 = {A, I} where A is the key

Now for 3NF there should not be any transitive dependencies :

So there is only one transitive dependency in relation R4

A,D -> G, H

And H -> J

So R4 should be decomposed as

R41 = A,D, G, H where A, D is the key

R42 = H,J where H is the key

SO the final relations for 3NF are :

R1 = {A, B, D} where ABD is the key

R2 = {A, B, C} where AB is the Key

R3 = {B, D, E, F } where B, D is the key

R41 = A,D, G, H where A, D is the key

R42 = H,J where H is the key

R5 = {A, I} where A is the key

(Q4) Find the 3NF decomposition of the Relation Schema

R = {Faculty, Dean, Dept, Chairperson, Professor, Rank, Student}

with the set of functional dependencies :

Faculty -> Dean

Professor -> Rank, Chairperson

Student -> Department, Faculty, Dean

Professor, Rank -> Department, Faculty

Department -> Chairperson

Department -> Faculty

Dean -> Faculty

Ans)

$\{Faculty\}^+$ -> Faculty, Dean

$\{Professor\}^+$ -> Professor, Rank, Chairperson, Department, Faculty, dean

$\{Student\}^+$ -> Student, Department, Faculty, Dean, Chairperson

$\{Student, Professor\}^+$ -> student, professor, rank, chairperson, department, faculty, dean

Key = { Student, professor } = R1

R2 = {Professor, rank, chairperson, department, faculty, dean } where professor is the key

R3 = {Student, Department, Faculty, Dean, Chairperson} where Student is the key

Now R2 has partial dependency

Professor -> Rank, Chairperson

Professor, Rank -> Department, Faculty

And transitive dependency

Professor, Rank -> Department, Faculty, dean

Faculty -> dean

Therefore it needs to be decomposed into

R21 = { Professor, Rank, Chairperson } where professor is the key

R22 = {Professor, Rank, Department, Faculty} where professor, rank is the key

R23 = {Faculty, Dean } where faculty is the key

Now R3 has

Student -> Department, Faculty,

Department -> Chairperson

Faculty -> Dean

Therefore it needs to be decomposed into

R31 = {Student, Department, Faculty} where student is the key

R32 = {Department, Chairperson} where department is the key

R33 = {Faculty, Dean } where faculty is the key which is same as R23

So the final relations in 3 NF are

Key = {Student, professor } = R1

R21 = {Professor, Rank, Chairperson } where professor is the key

R22 = {Professor, Rank, Department, Faculty} where professor, rank is the key

R23 = {Faculty, Dean } where faculty is the key

R31 = {Student, Department, Faculty} where student is the key

R32 = {Department, Chairperson} where department is the key

(Q5) Suppose we have a relation ABCD with some FD's F as follows:

F = A, B -> C

C -> D

D -> A

Compute closures A^{+}, C^{+}, AB^{+}, AC^{+} and all functional dependencies that follow from F.

Ans)

$\{A\}^{+}$ -> A

$\{C\}^{+}$ -> C, D, A

$\{AB\}^+$ -> A, B, C, D

$\{AC\}^+$ -> A, C, D

All Functional Dependencies:

C -> C

C -> D

C -> A

C -> C, D

C -> C, A

C -> D, A

C -> C, D, A

A, B -> A, B

A, B -> A, B, C

A, B -> A, B, D

A, B -> D

A, B -> C

A, B -> A, B, C, D

A, C -> A, C

A, C -> D

A, C -> A, C, D

CONFLICT SERIALIZABILITY

(Q1) Determine whether the following schedule is conflict serializable or not

T1: R(x), T2:R(x), T1:W(x), T2:R(y), T3:R(z), T2:W(z), T3:W(x), T3:W(y),

T2:W(y), T3:W(z)

Ans)

T1	T2	T3
R(x)		
	R(x)	
W(x)		
	R(y)	
		R(z)
	W(z)	
		W(x)
		W(y)
	W(y)	
		W(z)

An edge will form in case of a conflict situation where

(1) Read before write on same item

(2) Write before read on same item

(3) Write before write on same item

If there is a cycle then it is not conflict serializable.

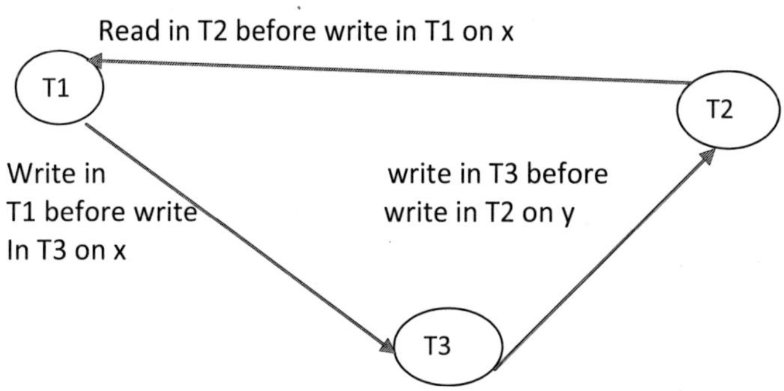

Forms a cycle, therefore not conflict serializable.

Index